Tamm's Textbo

AP* Psychology student workbook containing worksheets and course materials for use with:

Ciccarelli & White's

Psychology+

4th edition (white cover with orange goldfish)

Coursepak A   **Independently Made**

David Tamm

Contents

This resource book is organized in the following way to integrate with Ciccarelli & White's *Psychology 4th edition*:

"Perfect if there's a sub"

"A giant leap for studentkind"

"Awesome, usable resources!"

"Spend 1 hour's pay, save hundreds of hours of planning time!"

"Primary sources that are actually compelling and interesting"

"Engaging. Students pointedly interact with the book's features."

Copyrights

" When given as a full workbook, this material improves content coherency, student enjoyment, parent appreciation, and teacher satisfaction. Why? Because students have to read the actual book- the primary resource at hand for an AP* class. " - **AP* Teacher**

Suggested Use

Manic Moon Day
It is recommended that students have a lecture overview of the key points in each chapter, take notes, and discuss the concepts involved. Even though teachers are discouraged in some parts of the country from lecturing, the speed of the AP Psychology course necessitates some direct teacher-student transmission of content. Perhaps participation grades could be assigned for notes? Conversely, the Part I Exercise forms could be used as a guide during the discussion.

Textbook Tiw's Day
Most school districts encourage pair or group work. This can be used to positive effect if students mine the textbook or a review book in class and either jigsaw the chapter, presenting their take on part of the whole, or jointly venture to find the answers to the specific questions provided here in Part I, tailor made for each chapter. These can be given out as homework packets for a whole chapter at a time, or as individual assignments as the sections come up.

Writing Woden's Day
The AP* Psychology curriculum is reading and writing intensive, and a good way to build up the key thinking processes helpful in expressing oneself in writing is to brainstorm and diagram solutions to mini-FRQs appropriate to each chapter. Another helpful way to do writings is good old-fashioned reading comprehension, and as many teachers know, the content of the passages is key to student growth and success. If it ain't interesting, you might as well be pulling teeth at the dentist's office, even in an AP* class. Luckily, Psychology has great potential interest value. If you find the current work helpful and of high enough quality for the Monday and Tuesday assignments, you may want to obtain the companion volume to this book, *Tamm's Textbook Tools: The Grand Tour of Psychology* on *Amazon.com* or another platform. In it you will find FRQs, online assignments and short answers.

Technetronic Thor's Day
Many AP teachers try to bring technology into the classroom in the form of a laptop cart, or take students to a media lab, or even have them use their own mobile devices. *Kahoot.it* is popular as a Jeopardy-style review game, joining *Quizlet* flashcards and a vast number of other review materials available online. A good directory to psych websites usable with this class is in the addendum of this workbook. It includes the psychedelic 'groovy' site and *Psychsim* lab tutorials (though another publisher but available for anyone) with fully printable lab sheets for use with in a single class of computer time. Another index to these sites and more online is at Antarcticaedu.com/psy.htm. Also included in Part II of this volume is a Crash Course viewer-response sheet that can be given as homework on Thursday or completed as an in-class review assignment.

Fantastic Freyja's Day
It is suggested that students take a 50-question test once a week. That means many of the chapters will have to be cut in half and tests made on each half. If this happens on Friday, it is recommended students take home the Part I worksheets for homework, due the following week. Doing the vocab is a good way to introduce the new chapter, either at home with the book or by filling it in on Monday as class notes.

*These assignments work well as a homework battery

Suggested Year Plan

Ciccarelli & White's *Psychology* (2015) - Pearson
A modern approach

Engle's *Psychology* (1957) – Harcourt, Brace
A blast from the past

Week 1: chapter 1: history, approaches
Week 2: chapter 1: scientific attitude
Week 3: chapter 1: data collection
Week 4: chapter 1: correlation, experiments
Week 5: chapter 2: neurons
Week 6: chapter 2: brain
Week 7: chapter 2: brain, genes
Week 8: chapter 3: sensation, eye
Week 9: chapter 3: other senses, perception
Week 10: chapter 4: consciousness, sleep, dreams
Week 11: chapter 4: hypnosis, drugs
Week 12: chapter 5: classical conditioning
Week 13: chapter 5: operant conditioning
Week 14: chapter 6: memory
Week 15: chapter 7: cognition, language
Week 16: chapter 7: intelligence
Week 17: chapter 8: childhood development
Week 18: chapter 8: adult development
Week 19: chapter 9: motivation
Week 20: chapter 9: emotion
Week 21: chapter 10: stress
Week 22: chapter 10: social influence
Week 23: chapter 11: conformity, obedience
Week 24: chapter 11: groups, discrimination
Week 25: chapter 11: attraction, aggression, altruism
Week 26: chapter 12: Freudian personality
Week 27: chapter 12: trait theories, other
Week 28: chapter 13: anxiety disorders
Week 29: chapter 13: mood disorders, other
Week 30: chapter 14: psychotherapies
Week 31: chapter 14: biomedical therapies

chapter 1: problems of living, scope of psych
scientific method, fakery, appreciating psych
chapter 2: pseudoscience- astrology,
numerology, handwriting analysis, dreams,
hunches, "will", personality via appearances,
"unconscious mind," hypnosis, telepathy,
mind-reading, instincts.
chapter 3: how we learn, studies of learning,
training, thinking, remembering
chapter 4: easy vs. efficient learning,
improving learning, study periods, study aids,
examination techniques, suggestions
chapter 5: personality- its measurement
popular vs. scientific, traits, inventories
chapter 6: popularity and leadership
chapter 7: intelligence, measurements, IQ,
practicality, feeble-mindedness, superiority
chapter 8: heredity and environment, studies
great importance of environment, twin studies
chapter 9: nervous system, reaction time,
glands, emotional behavior
chapter 10: sensation and perception, vision,
color, hearing, other senses, aesthetics
chapter 11: mental health, high schoolers,
adjustment, frustration, conflict, reactions
chapter 12: emotional problems in high school
inferiority complex, thrill-seeking, daydreaming
dating, thoughts on sex, family conflicts
chapter 13: mental illness as a social problem
neurotic behavior, senility, drug addition,
epilepsy, other illnesses, treatments
chapter 14: friendship, romantic love
chapter 15: love and marriage, parents and
children, problem of discipline, fear, movies,
radio, television, comics, play, desirable toys
sex instruction for children
chapter 16: you and the world of work,
choosing a vocation, thinking as work,
efficient buying, psychology as vocation
looking ahead

Part I

Manic Monday
and
Textbook Tuesday

Vocabulary and
Class Assignment Sheets

Behavior
_____

Mental processes
_____

Description
_____

Theory
_____

Prediction
_____

Pic 5: Would you want to work in the kind of environment shown here?

_____

Describe the results of the experiment set up to test whether women were less interested in computer science due to environments like this one:

_____

Note the four goals listed for successful inquiry into psychological phenomena:

_____

Wilhelm Wundt
_____

Objective introspection
_____

Structuralism
_____

Functionalism
_____

Pic 6: How do you actually pronounce this guy's name in German?   *William Wundt*   *Vilhelm Voont*

Pic 7: Describe some memories and sensations you might experience if you smelled this rose:

       Memories (imagined, real)   *Sensations (smell, feelings)*

Natural selection
_____

Edward Titchener
_____

William James
_____

What was Harvard the first university in America to do? | What did James believe was important?

Charles Darwin

Darwin would most likely argue:

    a. We pick up behaviors and personality traits from interacting the world around us

    b. We inherit behaviors and personality traits that have had survival value for our ancestors

Mary W. Calkins

Francis Cecil Sumner

Of the six contributions to psychology by black researchers, which one do you think has the most lasting value?

                          Why?

Educational psychology

I/O psychology

Max Wertheimer

Gestalt

Cognitive psychology

Psychotherapy

Psychoanalysis

Sigmund Freud

Fig. 10: Are either of these a circle?

Pic 10: Would Darwin be surprised at Anna Freud's occupation? Why or why not?

What did Freud argue about the 'unconscious mind?'

Summarize: Is Freud still influential?

Do you believe in the existence of an 'unconscious mind'? Why or why not?

On a 1-10 scale, how important do you think a person's childhood memories are in the formation of their character?

Ivan Pavlov

Describe Pavlov's Dog experiment:

Which part of psychology do you prefer so far:

    a. The behaviorists' focus on observable behavior   *b. The psychoanalysts' focus on unconscious forces*

Behaviorism

John B. Watson

Mary Cover Jones

Reflex

Counterconditioning

Pic 11 (top): Describe the *Little Albert* Experiment	Do you think it was ethical to do this to a baby?	Would you volunteer *your* baby for this?

Pic 11 (bot.): Describe the results of the *Little Peter* experiment:

Phobia

Pg. 13 M/C: write the answer in the form of a statement. Underline the letter answer.

1.

2.

3.

4.

5.

PSYCHOLOGY NOW

They better have learned something after 100 years!

NAME_____

Note the basic characteristics of each of the following perspectives:

Psychodynamic

Behavioral

Humanistic
(esp. free will)

Cognitive

Sociocultural

Biological

Biopsychosocial

Evolutionary

B.F. Skinner

Eclectic

Pic 16: Joe was trapped in a vicious circle of negativity. Describe it graphically and label whether the traits or events indicate a biological, a psychological or a social issue:

List the subfields of psychology: | Pie Chart 17 (left): Draw where psychologists work:

Psychologist

Psychiatrist

Contrast *basic* versus *applied* research:

Pg. 19 M/C: write the answer in the form of a statement. Underline the letter answer.

1.

2.

3.

4.

5.

"I'm not a creeper... just doin' a little naturalistic observation"

Scientific method

Pic 20: Do *you* think kids who watch violence on TV (or online) are more likely to be aggressive than kids who do not *because they watch the shows*, or because -as kids predisposed to aggression- they are were just more interested in watching the violent shows in the first place? How sure do you consider yourself on this?

Relate the five steps of the scientific method:

1

2

3

4

5

_____

_____

_____

Why *should* you tell people if your experiment or research did *not* turn out to support your hypothesis?

Replication

Which is a more testable hypothesis?

a. *"Was there ever life on Mars?"*   b. *"What is the meaning of life?"*

Paradox: What if the meaning of *your* life is to find out the answer to the empirical question "Was there ever life on Mars?" Mind. Blown.

Naturalistic observation

Observer effect

Participant observation

Observer bias

Blind observer

Pic 23 (top): Is this person doing naturalistic observation? Why or why not?

Pic 23 (bot.): How different do you think the kids would act if they knew they were being watched?

Case study

Phineas Gage

Pic 24: How did this happen to Phineas Gage?

_____

Is it ethical to use people like this to further our understanding of psychological and medical science?

_____

Graphic 25: What does it mean to be a 'confederate' in a psych experiment?

_____

Would you rather be an 'actor' in a psych experiment or the 'writer' who writes the results?

_____

Survey _____

Population _____

Representative sample _____

Courtesy bias _____

Evaluate the strengths and weaknesses of each type of data gathering technique:

Technique	_Strengths_	_Weaknesses_

Pg. 26 M/C: write the answer in the form of a statement. Underline the letter answer.

1.

2.

3.

4.

5.

Attentiveness to this section is positively correlated with a good grade on the test.

Correlation

Variable

Correlation coefficient

Perfect positive correlation

Pic 28: Sketch in the five kinds of correlation scatterplots shown here- and yes, mark X and Y axes:

1

2

3

4

5

Which one is probably best representing the relationship between hours studying and test grades?

_____

Explain why 'correlation does not prove causation':

Give an example of a hypothesis question you might be able to test on students in your school:

Experiment

Operational definition

Write an operation definition for 'aggressive behavior': | Why is it important to explain it so thoroughly?

Independent variable

Dependent variable

What is the Hawthorne Effect? | Think of an example:
                                                  |
                                                  |
                                                  |

Experimental group

Control group

Random assignment

Placebo

Pic 31: If kids at your school were told they were getting a new super caffeinated drink that would make them excited and focused at the same time, and it was really just heavily sweetened yet tart fruit juice, do you think some would 'act crazy' 'cause they thought they were 'supposed to?'

Describe a time you remember when you either saw someone else or you yourself did something because it was expected of you and you wanted to fulfill the expectations, to the point the presence of the expectation became a self-fulfilling prophecy:

Experimenter effect

Single-blind study

Double-blind study

Stereotype

Pic 33: What do you think is the lesson of this story about the 'stereotype threat' experiment?

Statistics

Sample

Descriptive statistics

Measures of central tendency

Measures of variability

Frequency distribution

_____

Histogram

_____

Polygon

_____

If you are in class, take a quick class survey
of how many glasses of water everyone has
on an average day. Represent the results at
right (if you can't, then just copy the book):

Normal curve

_____

Skewed distribution

_____

Bimodal distributions

_____

Describe the differences in each of the following measures of central tendency:

Mean   *Median*   *Mode*

_____

Standard deviation

_____

Inferential statistics

_____

Statistical significance

_____

What is your opinion about the following examples on pg. 41:

    My Opinion   *My Reasoning*

1)

2)

t-test

_____

Significant difference

_____

Ethics

_____

Note the following ethical guidelines and the rationale for their existence:

1

2

3

4

5

6

7

8

If you had to eliminate one of these, which number do you think it would be? _____

Pic 44: What is the point of the joke in this comic?   Is there a real concern that animals are mistreated by man's experiments?

Critical thinking

Summarize the four pointers on thinking critically:

1

2

3

4

Pg. 46 M/C: write the answer in the form of a statement. Underline the letter answer.

1.

2.

3.

4.

5.

6.

7.

Multiple Choice: Write the answer in the form of a statement, underlining the letter.

1.

2.

3.

4.

5.

6.

7.

8.

9.

10.

11.

12.

FRQ.

_____

_____

_____

_____

_____

_____

_____

_____

Wait so neurons are what make up the Internet in my brain? Gee thanks neurons. ZAP! Just got another synaptic connection by thinking that!

Nervous system _____

Neuroscience _____

Biological psychology _____

Behavioral neuroscience _____

Neuron _____

Dendrite _____

Soma _____

Axon _____

Axon terminals _____

Glial cells _____

Graph 55: In the space below, sketch out the neuron and label the parts:

Myelin _____

Nerves _____

Multiple sclerosis _____

Ions _____

Diffusion _____

Channels _____

Sodium-potassium pump

Resting potential

Action potential

All-or-none firing

Polarization

Synaptic vesicles

Neurotransmitters

Synapse

Receptor sites

Graph 58 (top): Sketch the three diagrams showing the process of the electrical impulse as the sodium-potassium pump operates:

1)   2)   3)

Pic 59: What is this muscle about to do?   *Why* is it about to do that?

_____   _____

Graph 59: Sketch the synapse operating as it is in this diagram:

Excitatory vs. inhibitory synapse

Agonist

Antagonist

Pic 60: Why does the venom from this spider
make the human it bites go into convulsions? _____

Endorphins

Table 61: Note the key neurotransmitters and their functions:

Neurotransmitter	*Function*
1	
2	
3	
4	
5	
6	
7	

Huntington's disease

Reuptake

Enzymatic degredation

Graph 62: Why does cocaine cause people to feel 'high' and stimulated?

Describe what SSRIs are and why
they seem to improve people's moods:

Do you know anyone outside your psych class who might
benefit from knowing about how all this works with
drugs acting as agonists and antagonists for naturally
occurring brain chemicals? Will you tell them about it?

Pg. 63 M/C: write the answer in the form of a statement. Underline the letter answer.

1.

2.

3.

4.

5.

6.

(Use the space below to doodle and draw whatever comes to mind- just remember, it will be psychoanalyzed and possibly lead to your being diagnosed with pathological disease)

I'm nervous because I think my endocrine system is pumping out too much adrenaline and making me nervous. Oh no, it's happening again.

Graph 64: Sketch out the Nervous System chart, copying the arrows as it is on the page:

CNS _____

PNS _____

Spinal cord _____

Sensory neuron _____

Motor neuron _____

Interneuron _____

Pic 65: When the 80s band *Poison* sang a song called *Every Rose has its Thorn,* it was meant metaphorically- as in- every relationship (a rose) has rough or difficult times (its thorns). Is that why this lady is wincing? If not, why is she?

_____

Afferent is to _____

as efferent is to _____

Note the book's mnemonic device for remembering which is which:

Graph 65: When the 70s band *Moody Blues* sang a song called *Candle of Life,* it was meaning to remind us to take life easy and not to live too fast- or it might all be over before we even on our feet. Here someone is touching an actual candle. Draw the stages of their sensory experience:

Rate this mnemonic device: 1) helpful   2) eh   3) harder to remember than the original thing

Neuroplasticity

Psych in the News 66: Evaluate the four headlines:

Headline	Heard It? (Y/N)	Believe it? 3=yep, 2=maybe, 1=nope
1		
2		
3		
4		

Stem cells

Somatic nervous system

Autonomic nervous system

Sensory pathway

Motor pathway

Pic 68: Brain and spine are to _____

as nerves in the rest of the body are to _____

Pic 69: What part of the autonomic nervous system are these girls using?

_____

Sympathetic division

Parasympathetic division

Fight or flight reaction

Describe at least two times in your life when your 'fight or flight' reaction set in:

	Circumstances	Physiological changes
#1		
#2		

Graph 70: Now turn the page. Are any of the physiological changes you described here on the diagram?

These match what I said   *I didn't consider these but should have*   *I never had this happen*

Why do people tend to be hungry *after* a stressful or exciting situation is over, but not during?

_____

_____

The nervous system is in its essence: The endocrine system is in its essence:

a. electrical   b. chemical   c. both   *a. electrical   b. chemical   c. both*

Endocrine glands _____

Hormones _____

Pituitary gland _____ *located in:* _____

Oxytocin _____

Pineal gland _____ *located in:* _____

Melatonin _____

Thyroid gland _____ *located in:* _____

Thyroxin _____

Pancreas _____ *located in:* _____

Insulin _____

Glucagon _____

Hypoglycemia _____

Diabetes _____

_____

Gonads _____

Ovaries _____

Testes _____

Adrenal glands _____

Adrenaline _____

Corticoids _____

Cortisol _____

Chart 72: Sketch the endocrine glands:

Pic 73: Why is this person sticking themselves with a needle? Circle the term 'sugar' in your answer:

_____

Pg. 74 M/C: write the answer in the form of a statement. Underline the letter answer.

1.

2.

3.

4.

5.

THE LIVING BRAIN

You are about to get your head examined.

Lesion

ESB

DBS

Seizure

TMS

tDCS

CT scan

MRI scan

fMRI scan

EEG

Pic 76: How comfortable would you be getting this brain scan procedure done?

3=No problem   *2=Maybe*

1=Looks too weird   *0=No way!*

Pic 77: What is going on in each of these scans?

a.   *b.*

c.   *d.*

e.

MEG scan

PET scan

Pic 78: Have you ever seen any of these scans on a medical show on TV or in a movie? What happened? _____

Hindbrain

Medulla

Pons

Reticular Formation

RAS

Cerebellum

Pic 80: Sketch and label the following from this diagram:

1) Brain stem (hindbrain):

2) Limbic system:

(add the other parts on pg. 82)

3) Cerebellum:

Pic 81: What about this guy's job is requiring him to use his cerebellum?

_____

_____

Think of other jobs requiring intense use of the cerebellum:

_____

_____

The following animal has a stronger cerebellum:

a. tiger

b. turtle

Basil ganglia _____

Limbic system _____

Thalamus _____

Olfactory bulb _____

Hypothalamus _____

Hippocampus _____

Amygdala _____

Cingulate cortex _____

Pg. 84 M/C: write the answer in the form of a statement. Underline the letter answer.

1.

2.

3.

4.

5.

The Cortex
_____

Cerebral hemispheres
_____

Corpus callosum
_____

Pic 85 (top): What is different about these brains as they increase in complexity?

Sketch the lobe diagram on pg. 85 and label:

Occipital lobe
_____

Visual cortex
_____

Parietal lobe
_____

Somatosensory cortex
_____

Temporal lobe
_____

Auditory cortex
_____

Frontal lobe
_____

Pic 87: If this boxer is knocked down and conks the back of his head on the ring post, he might 'see' stars. Why?

_____

Have you ever 'seen stars'? What happened?

_____

_____

Motor cortex
_____

Mirror neurons
_____

Association areas
_____

Broca's area
_____

Aphasia
_____

Wernicke's area
_____

Paul Broca
_____

Carl Wernicke
_____

Cerebrum
_____

Hemispheric specialization
_____

What characteristics have you heard are 'left brained' as opposed to 'right brained'? Now check and copy your list agains the one on pg. 91:

Left	*Right*

Based on this data, do you think you are hemisphere-dominant? If so, which one? _____

Split-brain research
_____

Left hemisphere functions
_____

Right hemisphere functions
_____

Describe Gazzaniga's split-brain experiment:

Pg. 92 M/C: write the answer in the form of a statement. Underline the letter answer.

1.

2.

3.

4.

5.

6.

ADHD
_____

Multiple Choice: Write the answer in the form of a statement, underlining the letter.

1.

2.

3.

4.

5.

6.

7.

8.

9.

10.

11.

12.

FRQ.

_____

_____

_____

_____

_____

_____

_____

_____

_____

_____

SENSATION
I'm really feeling this today

Sensation _____

Stimuli _____

Transduction _____

Ernst Weber _____

JND _____

Weber's Law _____

Pic 100: Who knows how much extra sugar you would need. But the point is, would it be easier for your taste buds to sense a difference if your cup of coffee went from zero spoons of sugar to one, or from two to three spoons?

       a. from 0 to 1   *b. from 2 to 3*   Why? _____

Pic 101: In this feeble attempt to get you to go to the book website, you are being lured by the idea that a cool experiment with Weber's Law is ready to be demonstrated to you. So let's do that. Let's bite. Which of the two "circles of light" is darker?

                           a. the one on the left   *b the one on the right*

Absolute threshold _____

Chart 101: note the absolute threshold for each sense

Sense	Absolute threshold
1st	
2nd	
3rd	
4th	
5th	
6th supernatural	"I see dead people"

Gustav Fechner _____

Subliminal

Relate the story of how James Vicray was and what he taught us about subliminal messages:

Who:

What:

When:

Where:

Why:

How:

Habituation

Sensory adaptation

Pic 102: Did you always wonder, when you looked at people with lots of piercings, "wow doesn't that hurt?"

     a. actually, yeah I did wonder about that   b. no   c. why, I myself have many piercings

So why doesn't it (after a while, of course):

In 1985, two teenage guys smoked pot and drank a lot. Late into the night, after listening to *Stained Class,* an album by the band Judas Priest, they shot themselves. The parents sued the band in court, and the prosecutor, according to *Rolling Stone Magazine*, played a few Judas Priest songs for the judge forward and backward, trying to demonstrate Priest had 'backmasked' pro-suicide messages into their songs. If you were the lawyer for Judas Priest, how would you have argued to get the band off on the charges of inciting the suicides?

Pg. 103 M/C: write the answer in the form of a statement. Underline the letter answer.

1.

2.

3.

4.

Pic 104: Got crayons? Colored pencils? Markers? Reproduce the full spectrum below, taking care to get the visible light colors correct:

| | | | | | | | | | | | |

Photons _____

Brightness _____

Color _____

Saturation _____

Pic 105 (top): sketch out the eye and label the parts (but not their function):

Cornea _____

Aqueous humor _____

Iris _____

Pupil _____

Vitreous humor _____

Lens _____

Pic 105: What does the term 'refraction' mean in this context?

_____

Retina _____

Rods _____

Cones _____

Fovea _____

Blind spot _____

Pic 106 (top): How is nearsightedness different than farsightedness?

_____

_____

_____

_____

_____

Pic 106 (bot.): Sketch the detail of the parts of the retina:

Optic nerve _____

Visible spectrum _____

Visual accommodation _____

Bipolar neurons _____

Ganglion cells _____

Pic 107: Which hemisphere of your brain perceives what the left eye sees?

_____

What part of the brain is the visual cortex in?

_____

How many visual cortexes does a human being have?

_____

Dark adaptation _____

Pic 108: Aristotle taught the concept of the 'Golden Mean,' wherein people should strive to be harmonious in their actions. For example, if you were like this deer, caught in the headlights of an oncoming car, you might not do enough, do too much, or find the best way- the Golden Mean.

Match:

a. not acting enough

b. Golden Mean

c. acting too much

stepping out of the way

jumping in the ditch

freezing in fear

Light adaptation _____

Trichromatic theory
_____

Hermann von Helmholtz
_____

Opponent process theory
_____

Afterimages
_____

Color blindness
_____

Pic 109 (top): How does this image illustrate trichromatic theory?

_____

_____

_____

Pic 109 (bot.): Can you see the afterimage after staring like it says to do?

_____

Colors can get you in trouble if you don't know them or make them up, so be careful. Crayola found that out when people complained that its color _Flesh_ was only the flesh color of white people. So they changed it to _Peach_ in 1962. _Prussian Blue_ was changed to _Midnight Blue_ around the same time, and later, _Indian Red_ was changed to _Chestnut_, because people might have associated it with American Indians' skin color. From a psychological standpoint, do you think the changes were a good idea?

|_____

Pic 111: Draw the number you see in the following:

The left circle: _The right circle:_

Why is it mostly men that are colorblind?

_____

Pg. 112 M/C: write the answer in the form of a statement. Underline the letter answer.

1.

2.

3.

4.

5.

Comic 112: Why is this comic funny? Explain the joke because some people don't get it. To do this, you'll have to operationally define: 1. Dog, 2. Hearing, 3. Hertz

1   2   3

Wavelength _____

Hertz _____

Decibel _____

Outer ear _____

Pinna _____

Auditory canal _____

Middle ear _____

Hammer _____

Anvil _____

Stirrup _____

Graph 113: Copy the amplitude chart below: | On a Y-axis, chart the decibels from 1-135:
                                                   |
                                                   |
                                                   |
                                                   |
                                                   |
                                                   |
                                                   |
                                                   |
                                                   |
                                                   |
                                                   |

Inner ear _____

Cochlea _____

Hair cells

Auditory nerve

Pic 114: Draw the upper left 'ear' graphic, but make it bigger and label the parts from the other charts on it as well:

Place theory

Pitch

Frequency theory

Volley principle

Conduction hearing impairment

Nerve hearing impairment

Tinnitus

Cochlear implant

Pg. 117 M/C: write the answer in the form of a statement. Underline the letter answer.

1.

2.

3.

4.

5.

Hope your gate-control system is working alright- you gonna need it.

Gustation _____

Taste buds _____

Umami _____

Pic 118: Sketch the taste bud and label:

Olfaction _____

Olfactory sense _____

The very small- but still above absolute threshold for sight- woman on pg. 120 is asking whether she really has "skunk stink molecules" in her nose when she smells one around. But you know she is keepin' it clean, and "skunk" is a stand in for "fart." What she is really asking is, "you mean when I smell a fart then fart molecules are really in my nose? Gross!"

So, are they? _____

Pic 120: Draw the olfactory sense diagram on the right:

Somesthetic sense _____

Skin senses _____

Kinesthetic sense _____

Vestibular sense _____

Pacinian corpuscles _____

Free nerve endings _____

Somatic pain

Pic 121 (top): There is an interesting phenomenon related to the brain's neural plasticity going on here. When one sense is disabled, in this case sight, the brain will devote more gray matter to the other senses. One can get a feeling of this if one closes their eyes. All of a sudden, what you hear becomes more important to your brain. If you want to taste better, close your eyes while eating, like professional chefs do to 'savor' their creations. How is this concept illustrated in this picture?

Sketch below the skin graph on pg. 121 & label:

If you could shut off your pain receptors for a year and have no sense of touch at all, would you do it? why or why not?

CIPA

Phantom limb pain

Gate control theory

Sensory conflict theory

Pic 124: What would happen to his performer if his vestibular organs failed him?

Where is the vestibular organ?

Pg. 125 M/C: write the answer in the form of a statement. Underline the letter answer.

1.

2.

3.

4.

5.

PERCEPTION

"Figure this- you're grounded until you finish every last one of these vocab terms"

Perception _____

Cocktail party effect _____

Size constancy _____

Shape constancy _____

Pic 126: Which of the three, when you scan from left to right, gives you the most sense of shape constancy?

_____

Pic 127 (top): Are you able to 'reverse' the Necker Cube?

Yes   *No*   *I don't know*

Brightness constancy _____

Figure-ground _____

Reversible figures _____

Proximity _____

Similarity _____

Closure _____

Continuity _____

Contiguity _____

Pic 127: What do you see first?   *a. the people*   *b. the goblet*

Pic 128: Sketch in the five different gestalt principles of grouping:

Proximity   *Similarity*   *Closure*   *Continuity*   *Common Region*

Depth perception _____

Visual cliff _____

Pic 129: Answer the questions for further discussion relating to the Visual Cliff:

1.

2.

3.

4.

Monocular cues

Linear perspective

Relative size

Overlap (interposition)

Aerial perspective

Texture gradient

Motion parallax

Accommodation

Pic 130: Sketch a simple example of each of these pictorial depth cues:

a.   *b.*   *c.*   *d.*

Binocular cues

Convergence

Pic 131: Depth perception is important, as anyone who does a video search for *Mr. No Depth Perception snl* will know. What happens to vision when a person crosses their eyes? Sketch out the result:

Binocular disparity _____

Illusion _____

Feature deterctors _____

Hermann grid _____

Pic 132: What color dots do you see appearing at the intersections? _____

Muller-Lyer illusion _____

Pic 133: Which of the lines is longer in drawing a.? _____

Moon illusion _____

Pic 134: What causes the Moon Illusion? _____

Kitaoka rotating snakes _____

Pic 135 (top): When you see the snakes rotate, what direction do they rotate in?

     a. clockwise   *b. counter-clockwise*   *c. both*

Enigma illusion _____

Phi phenomenon _____

Perceptual set _____

Pic 136 (top): Who did you see first?   *a. the young woman*   *b. the old woman*

Top-down processing _____

Bottom-up processing _____

Pg. 137 M/C: write the answer in the form of a statement. Underline the letter answer.

1.

2.

3.

4.

5.

Parapsychology _____

Telepathy _____

Clairvoyance _____

Precognition _____

ESP _____

These controversial aspects of psychology fascinate people, and there is great debate about whether 1) mind over matter powers exist, 2) what forms they may take. What do you think about parapsychology?

_____

_____

Of the following, evaluate how much you agree that it has some credence, as in, that it might be real.

3 = I am almost sure it is real and that cases exist that demonstrate it.
2 = It might be real, I am not sure.
1 = I am almost sure it is not real and it has not been validated scientifically.

_____ **Telepathy**: Transfer of information on thoughts or feelings between individuals by means other than the five classical senses.

_____ **Precognition**: Perception of information about future places or events before they occur.

_____ **Clairvoyance**: Obtaining information about places or events at remote locations, by means unknown to current science.

_____ **Psychokinesis**: The ability of the mind to influence matter, time, space, or energy by means unknown to current science.

_____ **Near-death experiences**: An experience reported by a person who nearly died, or who experienced clinical death and then revived

_____ **Reincarnation**: The rebirth of a soul or other non-physical aspect of human consciousness in a new physical body after death.

_____ **Apparitional experiences**: Phenomena often attributed to ghosts and encountered in places a deceased individual is thought to have frequented, or in association with the person's former belongings.

Multiple Choice: Write the answer in the form of a statement, underlining the letter.

1.

2.

3.

4.

5.

6.

7.

8.

9.

10.

FRQ.

_____

_____

_____

_____

_____

_____

_____

_____

_____

_____

CONSCIOUSNESS   NAME_____

Hello, hello, is there anybody in there? Just nod if you can hear me- is there anyone home?

Consciousness _____

Waking consciousness _____

Altered state _____

Pic 145: Imagine driving a car on the main street near your school. Draw everything you could see, imagining all possible items competing for your sensory awareness out the front windshield:

Pic 146: Besides in your psych class, think of a place you fell asleep without meaning to. Analyze why it happened:

_____

_____

_____

How many hours on average do you sleep? _____

Circadian rhythms _____

Melatonin _____

Suprachiasmatic nucleus _____

Jet lag _____

Graph 148: At what age do human beings require the most sleep?

_____

How many hours does the average person need at:

6 _____   20 _____   50 _____   90 _____

Pic 148: Both of these people have sleep deprivation. Which one has a more vital function they could mess up on?

_____   Pic 149: Do lions worry about sleep?   Y   N

Microsleeps _____

Sleep deprivation _____

Adaptive theory _____

Restorative theory _____

Pg. 150 M/C: write the answer that is the right answer.

1.   2.   3.   4.   5.

Youtube: Silent Lucidity Queensryche. Then: Perfect Day Lou Reed. And the winner of "best song about sleep" is...

REM sleep _____

Non-REM sleep _____

Alpha waves _____

Beta waves _____

Theta waves _____

Delta waves _____

Pic 151: Sketch the wave patterns associated with each type:

Beta:

Alpha:

Theta:

Sleep Spindles:

Delta:

REM:

Hypnagogic images _____

Hallucination _____

Hypnic jerk _____

Sleep spindles _____

N1 _____

N2 _____

N3 _____

Sleep paralysis

REM rebound

Pic 152: sketch in the nightly pattern of a regular sleeping situation. Label the axes:

Pic 154: The function of the long duration of REM sleep in babies is, according to experts:

_____

Have you ever had a dream about being chased by a monster? What kind was it?

_____

Nightmares

Night terrors

Pic 155: If you were the judge in this dude's case, what would your verdict be? *guilty bigtime   not guilty*

After reading the other cases, what do you think about the discussion questions? Elaborate:

1)   2)

REM behavior disorder

Pic 156 (top)/157: Which comic do you think is funnier? _____

Chart 157: Copy the chart characterizing the various sleep disorders:

Pg. 158 M/C: write the answer in the form of a statement. Underline the letter answer.

1.

2.

3.

4.

5.

If you commit a crime in your dream, or even worse in someone else's dream, do the dream police come when you wake up?

Manifest content
_____

Latent content
_____

Pic 159 (top): How much, on a 1-10 basis with 10 being "always," do you buy into the idea that dreams are reflections of our lives in symbolic and direct storyline form?

_____

| Have you ever flown around in your dream? _____
| Aside from that, what other themes appear in your
| dreams?
|
|_____

Activation-synthesis
_____

AIM
_____

Chart 161: What kinds of meaning, if any, have you derived from your dreams?

_____

A theme in modern art around the middle of the 20th century when Dali painted *The Persistence of Memory,* was painting a dream. Recall an image from one of your dreams and draw it below:

Pg. 162 M/C: write the answer in the form of a statement. Underline the letter answer.

1.

2.

3.

4.

5.

Chart 162: Note the four stages of hypnotic induction:

1

2

3

4

On a 1-10 scale,
to what extent
do you think you

are hypnotizable?

_____

Hypnosis

Posthypnotic suggestion

Social-cultural theory

Table 164: What is the most surprising thing hypnosis can do, to you?	What is the most surprising thing it can't do?

Pic 164: How real does this look on a 1-10 scale? (10 = I would absolutely believe it: _____

Pg. 165 M/C: write the answer in the form of a statement. Underline the letter answer.

1.

2.

3.

4.

5.

Psychoactive drug _____

Physical dependence _____

Drug tolerance _____

Withdrawal _____

Psychological dependence _____

Have you known anyone you believe is addicted to a drug? What kind of addiction?

_____

People can only get addicted to illegal drugs:

True   *False*

Stimulants _____

Depressants _____

Hallucinogens _____

Amphetamines _____

Cocaine _____

Pic 168: You might have heard that Coca Cola used to have extract from the coca plant in it, the same plant from which cocaine is made.

What other kinds of uses did it have?

_____

Nicotine _____

Pic 169: What is this person's job?

_____

Does it surprise you that she is smoking?

_____

Is this illegal?

_____

Caffeine _____

If your teacher is drinking regular coffee, is your teacher technically on drugs? _____

Why did actor Heath Ledger die at age 28?

_____

Can you think of another famous person like him?

_____

Barbiturates _____

Benzodiazepines

Alcohol

According to Listal.com, the following famous people have alcohol use disorder: *Mel Gibson, Billy Joel, Stephen King, Robin Williams, Truman Capote, Lindsay Lohan, David Hasselhoff, Ernest Hemingway, Diana Ross, Dean Martin, Tracey Morgan, Robert Palmer, Amy Winehouse, Eddie Van Halen, William Shatner, Melanie Griffith, Elton John, Anthony Hopkins, Steven Tyler, Eminem, Mackenzie Phillips, Robert Downey Jr., Mickey Mantle, Billie Holiday, Orson Welles, Johnny Cash, Charles Bukowski, Alex Trebek, Frank Sinatra, Edgar Allan Poe, Samuel L. Jackson, Buzz Aldrin, Dick Van Dyke, Ben Affleck,* and *Michael J. Fox.* Others historically include *Beethoven, Churchill, Byron, William the Conqueror, Gerard Depardieu, Dickens, Ben Franklin, Yuri Gagarin, Andre the Giant, Van Gogh, Alexander the Great, Peter the Great, Vaclav Havel, Magellan, Picasso, Rasputin, Babe Ruth, Stalin, Tchaikovsky, Tesla, Mark Twain, Yeltsin, Bette Davis, Jim Morrison,* and *Pushkin.*

Of these, how many have you heard of?   How many have walked on the Moon?   Do you know any alcoholic people?

_____   _____   _____

What is 'binge drinking' and why does it lead to drunk driving, alcoholism and death?

| Table 172: What three types of drink are there?

| *type*   *percent alcohol*

|

|

|

|

|

|

Note the most important effect of in each drink category using Table 172:

   Number   *B.A.L.*   *Behavior*

Narcotics

Opium

Morphine

Heroin

LSD

MDMA (Ecstasy)

Marijuana

Chart 174: Note the adverse effects of each drug:

Stimulants   *Class/Name*   *Adverse Effect*

Depressants

Hallucinogens

Pg. 176 M/C: write the answer in the form of a statement. Underline the letter answer.

1.

2.

3.

4.

5.

6.

Multiple Choice: Write the answer in the form of a statement, underlining the letter.

1.

2.

3.

4.

5.

6.

7.

8.

9.

10.

FRQ.

_____

_____

_____

_____

_____

_____

_____

_____

_____

_____

_____

Learning

Pic 182: What lesson do you think this person has learned as a result of the situation as shown?

Pic 183: It says Pavlov was a physiologist. How is that different than a psychologist?

_____

_____

Maturation _____

Reflex _____

Stimulus _____

Response _____

Classical conditioning _____

US _____

UR _____

CS _____

CR _____

Pavlov's dog _____

Generalization _____

Discrimination _____

Pic 184 (top): Why are these kids salivating?

What kinds of stimuli might you salivate over?

_____

_____

Figure 184: Sketch in the Pavlov dog experiment using the arrows as shown:

    Before   *During*   *After*

Pic 185: In the case of the anxious dental patient, what items are the conditioned stimulus (CS):

_____

Graph 185: Summarize what the graph shows about the strength of the generalized response:

_____

Extinction

_____

Spontaneous recovery

_____

Pic 187: Sketch the graph for Extinction and Spontaneous Recovery below:

Higher-order conditioning

_____

Pic 187 (bot.): What is the additional step taken in this chart, which built off the previous chart on 184?

_____

_____

Pg. 188 M/C: write the answer in the form of a statement. Underline the letter answer.

1.

2.

3.

4.

5.

Little Albert

CER

Vicarious conditioning

Pic 189 (top): What is Little Albert being conditioned to fear?

_____

Why did Little Albert (no relation to Fat Albert) begin to fear these previously neutral stimuli?

_____

Pic 189 (bot.) These kids are probably feeling ___ as they wait in line for their vaccination.

a. happy   *b. angry*   *c. apprehensive*

Taste aversion

Pic 190: Push the play button on this picture with your finger. Did anything happen?

Y   N

What did you learn from this conditioning experience?

_____

Pic 191: The birds who are not eating this moth are primarily using this sense to find their food:

a. smell   *b. sight*   *c. hearing*

Pg. 192 M/C: write the answer in the form of a statement. Underline the letter answer.

1.

2.

3.

4.

5.

"Right this way to the Skinner box" (Footsteps echoing). "Ah yes here we are. Now go ahead, get inside..."

Operant conditioning _____

Edward Thorndike _____

Puzzle Box _____

Graph 193: Why might one surmise that Thorndike's cat got lucky on the second attempt?	How many attempts were needed before the cat really learned how to get out of the box?

B.F. Skinner _____

Skinner Box _____

Law of Effect _____

Reinforcement _____

Primary reinforcer _____

Secondary reinforcer _____

Positive reinforcement _____

Negative reinforcement _____

Pg. 196 M/C: write the answer in the form of a statement. Underline the letter answer.

1.

2.

3.

4.

5.

"I'll take my positive reinforcement on a fixed interval schedule please."

Partial reinforcement _____

Continuous reinforcement _____

Fixed ratio schedule _____

Variable ratio schedule _____

Fixed interval schedule _____

Pic 196: What is happening here that makes it a good illustration of *fixed interval* reinforcement?

Note a good example of a variable ratio reinforcement schedule

_____   _____

Pic 197: Why is this comic funny?

What kind of reinforcement schedule is being employed?

Pic 198: Note the pattern produced by the four reinforcement schedules- label the axes as well

a. fixed interval

b. variable interval

c. fixed ratio

d. variable ratio

Variable interval schedule _____

Pic 199: What kind of schedule is fishing?

Pic 199 (bot.): What kind of schedule is a slot machine?

_____   _____

Punishment _____

Negative punishment _____

Name	Kind of Reinforcement	Reason it is this kind
Arnie		
Trey		
Allen		
An Li		

Table 201: Note the ways to modify behavior:

	Reinforcement	Punishment
Positive		
Negative		

Pic 201: Why do you think this
girl's dad is making her do this? _____

Table 202: Note the following differences:

Examples of Negative Reinforcement	Examples of Negative Punishment

What are some arguments against using too much punishment to modify behavior?

1

2

3

4

Note three ways to make punishment more effective:

1

2

3

Discriminative stimulus

Shaping

Successive approximation

What kind of conditioning methods were used to train the dog pictured here?

_____

What kinds of things does the pictured dog do?

|

|

|_____

Instinctive drift

How does the raccoon's situation illustrate the power of nature over nurture?

_____

_____

Answer the Discussion Questions:

1

2

3

Token economy

Behavior modification

ABA

Biofeedback

Neurofeedback

Pg. 210 M/C: write the answer in the form of a statement. Underline the letter answer.

1.

2.

3.

4.

5.

"This means if I cheat off someone's paper, I'm just observing what they are learning... right?"

Tolman maze

Pic 211: Is this the most *amazingly* funny comic you have ever read?   Y   N

Latent learning

Maze 212: The minimum number of curtains an adept rat would have had to go through is

What were the results of this experiment?

_____   _____

Graph 213: Sketch the graph of the Tolman results at right:

Pic 213: What is this chimpanzee do to the astonishment of the researchers? Why did he or she do it?

What:_____ |

Why:_____ |

Wolfgang Kohler

Insight

Martin Seligman

Learned helplessness

Pic 214: What did the dog that had a 'safe space' do?   What did the dog that had no 'safe space' do?

_____   _____

(Whatever you do, don't Youtube: South Park Safe Space)

Have you ever learned to be helpless and said something like, "It's no use, I can't do it?" When?

_____

When the Apollo XIII astronauts had a fire in the spacecraft on the way to the moon (that's when the commander famously said, "Houston, we have a problem") there was almost no chance they would get back to earth alive. Look up how they did. Were they victimized by learned helplessness?

| Answer the question in big font on the bottom
| of pg. 214:

Albert Bandura

Observational learning

During the 'Bobo Beatdown,' as *Crash Course* rather humorously calls it, how did observational learning influence the boys' decisions?

_____

_____

_____

_____

_____

Pic 216: Pick your favorite scene from the Bobo Beatdown and sketch it below. Underneath, discuss what this particular scene is showing, and how Bandura interpreted it:

Note the four elements of observational learning and an example of each:

1   -

2   -

3   -

4   -

Pg. 218 M/C: write the answer in the form of a statement. Underline the letter answer.

1.

2.

3.

4.

5.

Pic 219: Summarize the methods by which you could get your cat to use the human bathroom:

Multiple Choice: Write the answer in the form of a statement, underlining the letter.

1.

2.

3.

4.

5.

6.

7.

8.

9.

10.

FRQ.

_____

_____

_____

_____

_____

_____

_____

_____

_____

_____

Something seems eerily familiar about all this

Memory _____

Storage _____

Retrieval _____

Information processing model _____

PDP model _____

Levels-of-processing model _____

Pic 227: Aurelian Hayman's hyperthymesia allows him to do things that are different than the usual person. What are these powers?

The dude halfway down pg. 227 is asking an important question- which model is right? If he asked you that, how would you answer?

Pg. 228 M/C: write the answer in the form of a statement. Underline the letter answer.

1.

2.

Sensory memory _____

Graph 229 (top): Sketch out an abbreviated form of this memory flow chart:

Iconic memory _____

Eidetic imagery _____

Pic 230: What exactly is Picasso doing in this scene, and what kind of memory was he employing?

Give an example of someone's use of photographic memory:

| Pic 231: Give an example of someone's use of echoic memory:

Pic 231 (bot.): Note an example of the cocktail party effect from your own life:

How is short-term memory different than working memory?

Working memory

Digit-span test

Short-term memory

Chunking

Pic 233: Write your answers to the digit span test here:

Trial 1:   Trial 2:   Trial 3:

Trial 4:   Trial 5:   Trial 6:

Trial 7:

Maintenance rehearsal

Long-term memory

Pic 234: What is likely to happen to this pharmacist if someone interrupts her with an irrelevant question like: "How's your day going?"

Note a time you did *rote* learning:

Elaborative rehearsal

Implicit (procedural)

Explicit memory

Pic 236: Aside from shoe tying, what other kinds of things are implicit memories?

Anterograde amnesia

Retrograde amnesia

Semantic memory

Episodic memory

Semantic network model

Pic 238: Sketch the graph on LTM:

| Pic 239: The guy on 238 says he can't remember the planet names
| sometimes. Help him out by making a semantic network for them, using
| and if they are gas giants or rocky:
|
|
|
|
|
|
|
|
|

If that guy had a problem recalling the names, would he have had as difficult a problem recognizing the names from a list? Would you? Circle the names of planets and dwarf planets in the Sol system:

Bajor	Earth	Vulcan	Mars	Mercury	Ceti Alpha V	Neptune
Terra Nova	Jupiter	Delta IV	Betazed	Tholia	Ferenginar	Eris
Pluto	Venus	Andoria	Makemake	Risa	Rura Penthe	Sedna
Kronos	Quaoar	Uranus	Romulus	Ceres	Alpha Centauri Bb	Cardassia

Prospective memory

Pg. 240 M/C: write the answer in the form of a statement. Underline the letter answer.

1.

2.

3.

4.

5.

"Retrieve Fido, retrieve! Run across that field, and retrieve all my life's memories!" What, you don't name your neurons?

Retrieval cue
_____

Encoding specificity
_____

State-dependent learning
_____

Pic 242 (top): What do you think the Sargent told him to get?

_____

Pic 242 (mid): Louis Armstrong's *What a Wonderful World* is the top wedding song of all time, even though *All the Time in the World* is probably better. What will help these people remember 'their' song?

_____

Context-dependent learning
_____

Recall
_____

Recognition
_____

Pic 242 (bot.): Would you volunteer for this Experiment?

          Y   N

Cereal position effect is when a person is taken into the grocery store and given 30 seconds to memorize where *Fruity Pebbles, Grape Nuts* and *Corn Flakes* are.

          T   F

TOT phenomenon
_____

Serial position effect
_____

Primacy effect
_____

Recency effect
_____

Graph 244: Draw the Serial Position Effect chart below:

Pic 244: If interviewing for a job, where do you not want to be in the line?

First

Middle

Last

Elizabeth Loftus
_____

Comic 245: Why are these guys calling each other "good buddy" and "big fella"?

_____

Pic 245: What was the name of the video Loftus showed to the people?

_____

Would you and some others confederate to stage a similar video argument and bust into a classroom? If you want some ideas, Youtube: Class Interrupted and see what comes up.

_____

Questions 246:

1)

2)

Automatic encoding

Flashbulb memory

Pic 246: Is this person's death going to be a flashbulb memory for everyone or just a certain group of people?

_____

Think of 3 flashbulb memories that are personal to you, that you probably won't ever forget:

1

2

3

Place the following in chronological order:

_____ Assassination of JFK
_____ VJ Day
_____ Apollo lands on the moon
_____ September 11th attacks
_____ Trump announces candidacy

Pg. 247 M/C: write the answer in the form of a statement. Underline the letter answer.

1.

2.

3.

4.

5.

Constructive processing

Hindsight bias

Misinformation effect

False-memory syndrome

Pg. 251 M/C: write the letter answer.

1.   2.   3.   4.   5.

Pic 250: Oh did you *forget something* last section? Did you forget to comment on why this girl should or should not be hypnotized to extract data about an alleged crime she witnessed? That's okay. You can comment on it now, and get full credit:

Would you like to have the ability to remember everything like "the Human Google?" Why?

_____

_____

Forgetting curve

Hermann Ebbinghaus

Graph 253: Sketch out the forgetting curve and don't forget to label the axes:

Distributed practice

Encoding failure

Memory trace

Decay

STOP! Which stop sign is the right one? Circle its place at right.　　A　　B　　C

Pic 253: What might be a downside to remembering everything?　　D　　E　　F

_____　　H　　I　　J

Disuse

Proactive interference

Retroactive interference

Pic 254: Copy the charts.

Proactive　　　　　　　　　　　　　　　　*Retroactive*

Chart 254 (bot.): Note the reasons for forgetting.

	Reason	Description
1		
2		
3		
4		

LTP

Consolidation

Retrograde amnesia

Anterograde amnesia

Pic 257: What kind of amnesia would Damon be expected to get as a result of this collision?	Think back (no pun intended): Did you ever hit your head and forget what was going on? Falling off a bike or being in an accident might do it, or for many other reasons. What happened?

Alzheimer's disease

Electroconvulsive therapy

Infantile amnesia

Autobiographical memory

Pg. 260 M/C: write the answer in the form of a statement. Underline the letter answer.

1.

2.

3.

4.

5.

Multiple Choice: Write the answer in the form of a statement, underlining the letter.

1.

2.

3.

4.

5.

6.

7.

8.

9.

10.

FRQ.

_____

_____

_____

_____

_____

_____

_____

_____

_____

_____

_____

Thinking about thinking? Seriously? Now that's a concept!

Thinking / cognition

Quick: How many windows are there in your house? _____. Were you right? _____

Pic 266: Sketch the island on the left, and the reaction time v. distance on the right:

Mental images

Mental rotation

Before you turn the page, draw a dog here to the right:

Done? Now turn the page. Did your 'dog' match either of these two examples?

_____

Pic 269: Why is the platypus a 'fuzzy' natural concept?

_____

Concepts

Prototype

Think of a fruit. Which fruit did you imagine first? _____

Circle five fruits that readily match your prototype of the term 'fruit,' then box in or otherwise highlight five that do not:

Loquat	strawberry	jaboticaba	grumichama	mulberry
Cherry	peach	nectarine	guava	blueberry
Blackberry	raspberry	lychee	dragonfruit	mango
Plum	pitomba	seagrape	white sapote	atemoya
Longan	feijoa	pear	prickly pear	sugar apple
Grape	melonberry	pomegranate	avocado	goji berry
Abiu	fig	lime	persimmon	apple
Banana	plantain	miracle fruit	natal plum	jujube
Calamondin	passionfruit	lemon	tangerine	kumquat
Orange	papaya	starfruit	tomato	apricot

Schemas

Problem solving

Decision making

Trial and error

Pic 270: Think of a time you used the same trial and error style of problem solving that this girl is using:

When have you taken a shortcut to get a job done faster?

Mechanical solution

Algorithms

Heuristic

Representative heuristic

Availability heuristic

Pic 272 (top): Have we become too dependent on technology? What is your opinion on that?

Working backwards

Pic 272 (bot.): Note a time in your life you have used a heuristic:

During the Punic Wars, the Romans captured a Phoenician ship and brought it to their port. They took the advanced ship apart and reverse engineered it, figured out all the materials they needed, and had people go into the forest to obtain the exact materials for many new Roman ships- instant navy!

How is that like working backwards?

Insight

Pg. 273 M/C: write the answer in the form of a statement. Underline the letter answer.

1.

2.

3.

4.

Time to cogitate- which means shaking your head until an answer falls out*   **warning: do not try this at home*

Functional fixedness

Rate your creativity on a 1-10 scale: _____   Pic 274: Can you solve the string problem? _____

Pic 274 (bot.)
You have three
attempts at this.

Do it soldier!

```
*    *    *        *    *    *        *    *    *
*    *    *        *    *    *        *    *    *
*    *    *        *    *    *        *    *    *
```

Pic 275: Why did this train operated by Robert Sanchez
in California run head on into another one in 2008?   _____

Mental set

Framing

Confirmation bias

Creativity

Convergent thinking

Divergent thinking

Table 276: Note the strategies for
stimulating divergent thinking:

1

2

3

4

Note the four Csikszentmihalyi
traits of creative people:

1

2

3

4

Pg. 277 M/C: write the answer in the form of a statement. Underline the letter answer.

1.

2.

3.

4.

Do you have enough of it to start right away without being told? Or do you need some negative reinforcement?

Intelligence _____

'g' _____

Charles Spearman _____

Howard Gardner _____

Multiple intelligences _____

Table 279: Note the nine types:

	Type	Description	Sample Occupation
1			
2			
3			
4			
5			
6			
7			
8			
9			

Of the above, which three do you think describe you the best?

1   2   3

Robert Sternberg _____

Triarchic theory _____

Analytical intelligence _____

Creative intelligence _____

Practical intelligence _____

Can you identify your own type of triarchic intelligence? Which is your strength?
_____

Alfred Binet

Stanford-Binet IQ test

IQ

Wechsler Test

Table 282: Looking at the four domains tested for by the WAIS, which do you *think* you would do the best in?

_____ because _____

Reliability

Validity

Normal curve

Table 283: Draw the bell curve and label the standard deviations:

| Pic 284: How *would* these two
| women talk about intelligence?
|
|
|
|
|
|

Standardization

Deviation IQ scores

Crystalized intelligence

Fluid intelligence

Cultural bias

Pg. 288 M/C: write the answer in the form of a statement. Underline the letter answer.

1.

2.

3.

4.

5.

Are you going to be a smart alec about this?

Intellectual development disorder
_____

DSM-V
_____

FAS
_____

Giftedness
_____

MENSA
_____

Pic 291: Would you join MENSA if given the opportunity?

Pic 291 (bot.): How did Terman redefine how people thought about intelligence?

_____

Lewis Terman
_____

Questions 293: Answer the questions on Terman:

1   2   3

Emotional intelligence
_____

Heritability
_____

Flynn Effect
_____

The Bell Curve
_____

Note Herrnstein and Murray's arguments versus the authors' opinion on IQ:

Herrnstein and Murray   *Authors' response*

Stereotype threat
_____

Pg. 297 M/C: write the answer in the form of a statement. Underline the letter answer.

1.

2.

3.

4.

"Speak Sparky, speak!" Arf arf, hou hou, woof, bark, grr... ruff ruff! "Good, now Sparky, did the noises you made influence the way you think?"

Language _____

Grammar _____

Noam Chomsky _____

Phonemes _____

Morphemes _____

Give an example of phonemes: Give an example of morphemes:

Syntax _____

Semantics _____

Pragmatics _____

Lev Vygotsky _____

Linguistic relativity hypothesis _____

Cognitive universalism _____

Do you think language constructs thoughts differently if one is thinking in a different language? _____

Pic 302: If you found out Kanzi beat you at an online video game, how would you feel?

Pg. 303 M/C: write the answer in the form of a statement. Underline the letter answer.

1.

2.

3.

4.

5.

Multiple Choice: Write the answer in the form of a statement, underlining the letter.

1.

2.

3.

4.

5.

6.

7.

8.

9.

10.

FRQ.

_____

_____

_____

_____

_____

_____

_____

_____

_____

_____

_____

Human development _____

Longitudinal design _____

Cross-sectional design _____

Cross-sequential design _____

Cohort effect _____

Table 311: Summarize the table to the point you know the differences between the types:

Cross-Sectional

Longitudinal

Cross-Sequential

Nature _____

Nurture _____

Answer the girl's question on 311- why do you think a person like Hitler would write so many anti-Semitic statements in *Mein Kampf* and wage a blitzkrieg war against Poland? To what extent are those aggressive actions attributable to his inherited traits, or to the circumstances in which he grew up and lived?

_____

_____

Behavioral genetics _____

Genetics _____

DNA _____

Gene _____

Chromosomes _____

Pic 312 (bot.): sketch a rung
of DNA, labeling the amines:

_____

Dominant _____

Recessive _____

Polygenic _____

Comic 313: Is this DNA molecule right? He, or rather it, is talking to some other kind of molecule that is much simpler in nature. Defend his statement to the simple molecule. What exactly are some of the things he has to remember? Use the first person for added effect, as if you were continuing the convo:

_____

_____

_____

Summarize the following:

Tay-Sachs _Down syndrome_ _Klinefelter's syndrome_ _Turner's syndrome_

Chart 314: Gregor Mendel discovered how traits are passed through the generations in the 19th century. Sketch out the two inheritance situations:

_a._

_b._

Pg. 315 M/C: write the answer in the form of a statement. Underline the letter answer.

1.

2.

3.

4.

5.

6.

Yeah... I remember when I was a one-celled organism, 'round 9 months before my birthday. That was the good day. Things were simple.

Fertilization _____

Ovum _____

Zygote _____

Monozygotic twins _____

Dizygotic twins _____

Pic 316: Sketch out the different paths determining whether the twins will be identical or fraternal:

Identical:

Fraternal:

Pic 317: The names of the conjoined twins shown here are _____ and _____.

Answer the questions stating your opinion after thinking about their situation realistically:

Q1)

Q2)

Germinal _____

Uterus _____

Placenta _____

Umbilical cord _____

Stem cells _____

Embryo _____

Critical period _____

Teratogen

Fetus

Pic 318: Measured in *days,* how long were you and the average person in each phase of development:

Germinal _____   Embryonic _____   Fetal _____

Table 319: Note the various teratogens, and if you know someone who is pregnant, make sure they know about these as well, as this is serious stuff for the health of the new baby:

	Teratogen	Effects of Development
1		
2		
3		
4		
5		
6		
7		
8		
9		
10		

Pic 321: What is the purpose of a sonogram?   Would you want to know whether the child will be a boy or girl when the time comes- or would you want it to be a surprise?

_____   _____

Pg. 320 M/C: write the answer in the form of a statement. Underline the letter answer.

1.

2.

3.

4.

5.

"Hi there little guy- let's talk about how schemas, assimilation and accommodation aid your cognition." "Hey, little guy? Wake up!"

Reflexes

Synaptic pruning

Pic 322: Note the five basic infant reflexes:

1

2

3

4

5

| Pic 323: Note the six motor milestones:

| 1

| 2

| 3

| 4

| 5

| 6

Cognitive development

Jean Piaget

Schemes

Table 324: Copy this important Piaget stages table below:

Stage	Age	Cognitive Development

Object permanence

Egocentrism

Centration

Conservation

Chart 326: Draw the two "answers" given by the preoperational child regarding conservation

a. the glasses   b. the pennies

Pic 326: What did Lev Vygotsky teach about how people learn?

Irreversibility _____

Scaffolding _____

ZPD _____

Child-directed speech _____

Cooing _____

Babbling _____

One-word speech _____

Two-word speech _____

Telegraphic speech _____

Pic 328: What is the purpose of a gesture?   Pic 329: What do _you_ believe about immunizations?

_____   _____

ADS _____

Immunization _____

Pg. 331 M/C: write the answer in the form of a statement. Underline the letter answer.

1.

2.

3.

4.

5.

"Is this all there is?" –Donald Trump after becoming a 10 billionaire.   *"Guess there's only one thing left to do."*

Temperament

Note the three kinds of temperament identified by Chess & Thomas:

	Type	*Characteristics*
1		
2		
3		

Attachment

Note the similarities and differences between the following:

Unique to stranger anxiety	*Similarities*	*Unique to separation anxiety*

Note the four attachment styles promulgated by Mary Ainsworth:

	Type	*Characteristics*
1		
2		
3		
4		

Imprinting

Harry Harlow

Monkey Experiment

Summarize the Harlow Monkey Experiment's findings below, then answer the two questions:

1)

2)

Self-concept

Erik Erikson

Chart 336: The biggest chart in the book- Erikson's Psychosocial Stages. Guess what? Yep. It's important:

Stage	Crisis	Successful dealing	Unsuccessful dealing
1			
2			
3			
4			
5			
6			
7			
8			

Pg. 337 M/C: write the answer in the form of a statement. Underline the letter answer.

1.   2.   3.   4.   5.

Depending on who you are, you're going to want to skip this or you're going to be into it way too much. You know who you are.

Adolescence _____

Puberty _____

Primary sex characteristics _____

Secondary sex characteristics _____

Pic 338: What do you think caused these adolescent boys to speculate like this on their own increased interest in girls?

If some psychologists came up to you and said, "We're doing a sexual survey, do you mind participating?" You would:

a. agree   *b. say no*   *c. call the cops*

Growth spurt _____

Kinsey Study _____

Personal fable _____

Imaginary audience _____

The book says adolescents believe they are 'one of a kind'. Are they right or wrong? Defend your answer:

Do you remember a time you imagined an audience even though you were by yourself? Were you scoring a winning shot or doing something heroic?

Read and think about the moral dilemma on pg. 340. Now you are the ant. Do you give your food and shelter to the grasshopper, or not? Why yes or no?

The grasshopper has hired a lawyer and sued you for saying no because you worked hard and were responsible while the grasshopper was carefree, enjoyed the summer and didn't listen to you when you warned him. What *moral* argument do you think the lawyer might use to convince the judge to take your food and shelter and give it to the grasshopper?

_____

Are you prepared to watch the grasshopper die of frostbite?

_____

_____

Moral development

How do men and women tend to think differently about moral decisions?

Men   *Women*

Lawrence Kohlberg

Table 340: Sketch in Kohlberg's Levels of Morality with examples:

Level	How Rules are Understood	Example
1		
2		
3		

Comic 341: What is the meaning of the message in this comic?

Brainstorm other events from daily life that illustrate this competitive nature of masculinity:

_____

_____

_____

_____

Pic 341 (mid.): Do you believe differences in average ability in math between men and women is from:

nature/genetics   nurture/environment   both

Pic 341 (bot.): Cite evidence of desire to fit in from this picture:

_____

Pg. 342 M/C: write the answer in the form of a statement. Underline the letter answer.

1.

2.

3.

4.

5.

Menopause _____

Andropause _____

'Use it or lose it' _____

What are some bad lifestyle habits cited that young adults and adolescents sometimes have, that may not show obvious signs until the '40s or '50s?

_____

Pic 344: This lady is doing the following game:

_____

The benefit of this game to her is:

a. entertaining   *b. keeps brain active*   *c. both*

Authoritarian _____

Permissive _____

Authoritative _____

Now it's your turn to analyze your parental units. Rate each parental unit (which could be a mom, dad, step-mom, step-dad, grandparent, extended family member etc., whoever was 'around' that you had to deal with. You might add in a couple teachers just for fun.

Parental Unit   *Their style*   *Example behavior or attitude confirming style*

Pg. 347 M/C: write the answer in the form of a statement. Underline the letter answer.

1.

2.

3.

4.

5.

THEORIES OF AGING NAME_____

Ali G: "What are the chances that me will eventually die?"

Everett Koop, Surgeon General of the United States: "100%. I can guarantee you that. 100%. You will die."

Ali G: "I didn't realize you was a playerhater, I'd like to get a second opinion on that."

A lot of people are afraid of dying, even the thought of dying, or even the thought that eventually, everyone dies and a new generation will live upon the earth. Rate your comfort level with that thought:

a. *It is a scary thought*   b. *I try not to think about it*   c. *It's just reality, get over it*

Cellular clock
_____

Wear and tear theory
_____

Free-radical theory
_____

Activity theory
_____

Denial
_____

Bargaining
_____

Depression
_____

Acceptance
_____

"Someone once told me that time was a predator that stalked us all our lives. But I rather believe than time is a companion who goes with us on the journey, and reminds us to cherish every moment because they'll never come again. What we leave behind is not as important how we lived. After all, we're only mortal."

What is your perspective on time? Is it a predator or a companion?   -Captain Jean-Luc Picard

_____

Pg. 349 M/C: write the answer in the form of a statement. Underline the letter answer.

1.

2.

3.

4.

5.

Multiple Choice: Write the answer in the form of a statement, underlining the letter.

1.

2.

3.

4.

5.

6.

7.

8.

9.

10.

FRQ.

_____

_____

_____

_____

_____

_____

_____

_____

_____

_____

_____

_____

MOTIVATION

What do you think- should we get started on that motivation research or not?

Motivation

Brainstorm three things that motivate you on the weekend when you have more free time:

_____

| Pic 357: The purpose of ads is to try and _____ people to go out and spend their money.

| Is there money to be made in motivation?   *Y   N*

Extrinsic motivation

Intrinsic motivation

William McDougall

Instinct theory

How many of McDougall's instincts could you identify in yourself if you tried? Circle the ones you are for sure about or know enough about to understand or agree with:

1) Instinct of flight and emotion of fear

2) Instinct of repulsion and emotion of disgust

3) Instinct of curiosity and emotion of wonder

4) Instinct of pugnacity and emotion of anger

5) Instinct of self-abasement and emotion of subjection

6) Instinct of self-assertion and emotion of elation

7) The parental instinct and emotion of tenderness

8) Instinct of reproduction

Need

Drive

Primary drives

Secondary drives

Homeostasis

Pic 358: Everyone is "the kind of person" who is satisfied with satisfying primary drives like thirst-quenching, which we all have to do, but are you also "driven to do strenuous activities like play sports, explore in nature, run around all the time etc. when there is no physical need to do so"?

a. Not at all   *b. Not too much*   *c. Actually quite often*   *d. I always am physically active*

Chart 358: Sketch in the hunger chart:

Note the characteristics of the three major needs identified by David McClelland:

Affliction	*Power*	*Achievement*

Pic 359: Predict how the same need for power Puff Daddy displays in his behavior of purchasing things in excess of what he needs or even newer versions of what he already has, might manifest itself in his relationships with wives, employees and friends:

If you had a lot of money- not unlimited but a lot- how do you think you would spend or not spend it? Would you spend it like Puff Daddy?

_____   _____

Internal locus of control

External locus of control

Contrast Carol Dweck's theory of motivation from David McClelland's:

Dweck	*McClelland*

Pic 360: "Knowing the answer" is a good feeling. You know. You <u>know</u>. And now its time that everyone else knows you know too. The implication in this picture is that the girl will be positively reinforced by her teacher's praise and be even more attentive and interested- good characteristics of learners, of course- and that she will get caught up in a virtuous cycle. Do you agree? *Why* do you care about school?

Pg. 361 M/C: write the answer in the form of a statement. Underline the letter answer.

1.

2.

3.

4.

5.

No it's not THAT kind of arousal you dirty animal! Okay that may be part of it. But there's a lot more. Seriously. Not really.

Stimulus motive
_____

Arousal theory
_____

Optimum arousal
_____

Yerkes-Dodson law
_____

Graph 361: What does this chart actually *mean?*   Pic 362: How much fun does this look like to you?

_____   *a. I need to do that right now*   *c. no. never. ever.*

_____   *b. I'd try it on a dare or for $$$ but it looks scary*

Sensation seeker
_____

Hedonism
_____

Table 362: Answer the questions YES or NO

1   2   3   4   5   Result:

Incentives
_____

Incentive approaches
_____

Abraham Maslow
_____

Hierarchy of needs
_____

Physiological needs
_____

Safety needs
_____

Belongingness needs
_____

Esteem needs
_____

Cognitive needs
_____

Aesthetic needs
_____

Self-actualization needs
_____

Transcendence needs

Table 364: Sketch out the Hierarchy of Needs below:

Peak experiences

Pic 365: First of all have you seen the movie *Castaway?*

Do you think you can convince your teacher to show a 3 hour movie in class and burn a week up because it obliquely is related to this chapter on motivation?　　*Y*　　*N*

Self-determination theory

Individualist culture

Collectivist culture

Pic 366: If "Bill" has a respect for objective knowledge and is not a status or award seeker, will he be angry at the teacher for not rewarding him but instead telling it like it is?

What *is* the reward you eventually get for doing all this work in all these classes at school for 13 or so years?

Pg. 368 M/C: write the answer in the form of a statement. Underline the letter answer.

1.

2.

3.

4.

5.

Ah yes, food. That weird mushy stuff we eat. So is "you are what you eat" true? I mean, elementally speaking?

"Great meals fade in reflection. Everything else gains. You know why? Because it's only food- the stuff we put in us. Keeps us going. It's only food."

                             Ricky Roma (Glengarry Glen Ross, 1993)

Are you the kind of person who agrees with Mr. Ricky Roma and considers food just a utility to be consumed in order to "keep you going," or are you the kind of person who, as is commonly said of French people, demands to savor delicious or gourmet foods as an important part of your life and culture?

_____

| What are some of your favorite foods?

Do you recall what you've eaten for the past week? Was Ricky Roma right and it just fades?

Today Breakfast	*Snack 1*	*Lunch*	*Snack 2*	*Dinner*
Yesterday Breakfast	*Snack 1*	*Lunch*	*Snack 2*	*Dinner*
2 days ago Breakfast	*Snack 1*	*Lunch*	*Snack 2*	*Dinner*
3 days ago Breakfast	*Snack 1*	*Lunch*	*Snack 2*	*Dinner*
4 days ago Breakfast	*Snack 1*	*Lunch*	*Snack 2*	*Dinner*
5 days ago Breakfast	*Snack 1*	*Lunch*	*Snack 2*	*Dinner*
6 days ago Breakfast	*Snack 1*	*Lunch*	*Snack 2*	*Dinner*
7 days ago Breakfast	*Snack 1*	*Lunch*	*Snack 2*	*Dinner*

Circle the three healthiest things you ate.
X out the three unhealthiest things you ate.

Is thinking about it helping make you more self-conscious about what you eat?

Insulin

Glucagon

Leptin

Hypothalamus and hunger

Set point

Pic 368: What did the researchers do to the rat on the right to make it not know when to stop chowing?

Table 269: What happens to the amount of food you need to eat to maintain your average body weight- as people age?

Basal metabolic rate

Obesity

Pic 370: Compare why Japanese women eat with why American women eat, generalization aside:

Pic 371: If these people's genetic relatives in Europe are 2/3 of their weight, make a case that some of this is environmental in nature

Anorexia

Bulimia

Binge-eating disorder

Pg. 375 M/C: write the answer in the form of a statement. Underline the letter answer.

1.

2.

3.

4.

5.

6.

7.

8.

9.

Emotion

Amygdala and emotion

Pic 377: Sketch below the 'low road' and 'high road':

| Contrast the low road with the high road,
| referencing LeDoux' work:

Universal expressions

Pic 379: Note the six universal expressions and try to draw them the best you can:

Paul Ekman

Display rules

The three elements of emotion are:	An example is:

1

2

3

Chart 381 (top): Sketch the Common Sense Theory of Emotion below:

James-Lange theory

Chart 381 (bot.): Sketch the James-Lange Theory below:

Cannon-Bard theory

Chart 382: Sketch the Cannon-Bard Theory below:

Schachter-Singer theory

Chart 383 (top): Sketch the Schachter-Singer Two-Factor Theory below:

Facial feedback theory

Chart 383 (bot.) Sketch the Facial Feedback Theory below:

Cognitive-Mediational theory

Chart 381 (bot.): Sketch the Cognitive-Mediational Theory below:

Pg. 384: The Angry/Happy Man. Read and answer the questions:

1

2

3

4

Pg. 385: Do *you* believe in facial feedback? Is laughing contagious? Try smiling at someone and see what happens. Try it on your neighbor. What happened?

Pg. 387 M/C: write the answer in the form of a statement. Underline the letter answer.

1.

2.

3.

4.

5.

Pg. 388. What is GTD?

Multiple Choice: Write the answer in the form of a statement, underlining the letter.

1.

2.

3.

4.

5.

6.

7.

8.

9.

10.

FRQ.

_____

_____

_____

_____

_____

_____

_____

_____

_____

_____

I ain't afraid of no ghosts (cue Ghostbusters theme)

Pic 394: Before beginning this section, let's brainstorm what you and others see as stressors in a high school student's life:

Stressors you specifically have   *Stressors other students have*

Stress
_____

If you were offered the opportunity to do a 10-page research paper in the last week of the semester, would you

a. Not do it- not worth it   *b. Do it but be totally stressed out*   *c. Do it because it's an opportunity*

Stressors
_____

Distress
_____

Eustress
_____

Catastrophe
_____

Major life change
_____

Hassles
_____

Table 397: Tabulate your stress by adding all the life change units that apply to you on the SRRS:

_____

What does SRRS stand for?

_____

Since the list is incomplete, you'd have to finish online to get their prediction about the amount of stress you are going through. But will everyone be affected by similar stress levels to the same degree?

Y   N

Pg. 399 M/C: write the answer in the form of a statement. Underline the letter answer.

1.

2.

3.

4.

5.

Time to get worked up about this

Pressure _____

Frustration _____

Aggression _____

Frustration-aggression principle _____

Displaced aggression _____

Scapegoats _____

Escapism _____

Withdrawal _____

Pic 400: For what stress-related reason are nursing homes presented here in a good light here?

_____

Pic 401: What kind of aggression is claimed as being in play in this picture?

_____

Provide a summary and real world example of each of the following conflicts:

Approach-approach   *Approach-avoidance*

Avoidance-avoidance   *Double approach-avoidance*

Multiple approach-avoidance conflicts _____

Pg. 403 M/C: write the answer in the form of a statement. Underline the letter answer.

1.

2.

3.

4.

5.

Right-mind lower stress. Good for immune system. So are zinc, aloe and garlic –Attributed to the Buddha Gautama

GAS

Note the role of each of the following in General Adaptation Syndrome:

Alarm   *Resistance*   *Exhaustion*

Graphic 405: Draw a stick figure of the fireman shown here and label the physiological stressors:

Alarm   *Resistance*   *Exhaustion*

Immune system

Psychoneuroimmunology

Question 406: Make the case that there is a 'good' stress and a 'bad' stress:

When is stress good   *When is stress bad*

Are increased chances of getting a cold positively or negatively correlated with elevated stress levels?

_____

CHD

Good cholesterol

Bad cholesterol

Type 2 diabetes

Chart 407: Sketch in the chart, with the word 'stress' in the 'stress box' bigger to reflect its centrality:

NK cell

Pg. 408 Issues in Psychology: Answer the questions.

1

2

Primary appraisal

Secondary appraisal

Chart 410: Sketch the paths of the responses to a stressor. You can do it horizontally if you want:

Type A personality

Type B personality

Comic 411: Which personality is being made fun of here?   Graph 411: Who is most at risk for CHD?

Type C personality

Neuroticism

Type H personality

Type Z personality?

Can you think of anyone you know personally (family, friends, teachers) *or* people you know indirectly (media personalities, politicians, TV, movies, music, sports etc.) that display elements of a personality?

	Type A	*Type B*	*Type C*	*Type H*	*Type Z*
P					*(See Comic 413)*
E					
O					
P					
L					
E					

In general, how do each of the personalities deal with "getting lemons thrown at them"?

Type A	*Type B*	*Type C*	*Type H*

Optimists

Pessimists

How did Martin Seligman summarize how optimism affects people's long-term lives?

1)

2)

3)

4)

Pg. 415 M/C: write the answer in the form of a statement. Underline the letter answer.

1.

2.

3.

4.

5.

"I had the right of way! You cut me off!" That's it I'm getting out of this car! So is he! I'm gonna hit him! "Hey dude, you need a hug."

What kinds of stress factors are associated with the following items:

    Road rage   *Living in poverty*   *Job*

Pic 415: These Afrikaner children live in a squatter camp in Africa. Youtube: *Journeyman Pictures South Africa Poverty.* What kind of stress may come from the conditions in which they live?

_____

Burnout

_____

Question 416: Do you agree that what the book calls job stress, or workplace stress, is for many students equivalent to school stress?

_____

Pic 416: These Buddhists are said to be "maintaining some of their former cultural traditions" in California while wearing popular Western clothes. What would be most equivalent?

a. European Christians building homes in Paraguay
b. Muslims in China wearing Islamic clothing styles

Acculturation
_____

Integration
_____

Assimilation
_____

Separation
_____

Marginalization
_____

Social-support system
_____

Lupus
_____

Pg. 418 M/C: write the answer in the form of a statement. Underline the letter answer.

1.

2.

3.

4.

5.

Coping strategy

Problem-focused coping

Emotion-focused coping

Pic 420: These guys are coping by

How do you cope on an everyday basis? Do you do this too?

_____

_____

Pic 420 (bot.) Have you ever tried yoga, meditation or prayer? And did it help relax you? _____/_____

How about listening to music? Hanser and Thompson describe in *Effects of a Music Therapy Strategy* (2007) the following benefits of music therapy:

- Listening to classical music.
- Listening to music of one's choice and introducing an element of control to one's life.
- Listening to music that reminds one of pleasant memories.
- Listening to music as a way of bonding with a social group.
- Not listening to types of music that are associated with being loud or angry, such as metal.

Let's take these one at a time. What's the last Classical music piece you've listened to?

When or what song were you listening to that made you feel you had some degree of control over your life?

_____

_____

What is the last song that reminded you of a pleasant memory (mood elevation)?

When have you realized you like a song more because You associated it with hanging out with friends?

_____

_____

*The oldest vocal music, *Gregorian Chant,* was "rediscovered" in the 1990s to have a secular stress-relieving effect and became a surprise selling phenomoneon. The monks of Santo Domingo de Silos Monetary in Spain recorded albums called Chant, Chant II and Chant III. Youtube it!*

Meditation

Concentrative meditation

Progressive muscle relaxation

Visualization

Pg. 423: Answer the questions

1

2

Multiple Choice: Write the answer in the form of a statement, underlining the letter.

1.

2.

3.

4.

5.

6.

7.

8.

9.

FRQ.

_____

_____

_____

_____

_____

_____

_____

_____

_____

_____

Conform. Obey. Whatever you do, do not Youtube the following: They Live Sunglasses

Social psychology

Social influence

Conformity

Solomon Asch

Pic 428: Do you think there really are people who follow the norms of the community like this sheep does?

a. No

b. Yes- and I remember that Conventional Stage of Kohlberg's morality theory too

Chart 429: Carefully copy Ashe's lines:

Standard   *Comparison(s)*

Normative social influence

Informational social influence

Groupthink

Pic 430: How were each of the following sad examples of groupthink?

Titanic sinking	*Bay of Pigs Invasion*	*Challenger exploding*	*Horizon rig oil spill*

Group polarization

Social facilitation

Social impairment

Chart 431: Note the characteristics of groupthink:

	Characteristic	Description
1		
2		
3		
4		
5		
6		
7		
8		

Social loafing

Deindividuation

Pic 432: Do you like group work in school? Educrats sure love it. Think of a time in school when someone in your group- when you had to do group work and actually cooperated- was socially loafing:

Similarly, think of a time when you felt deindividuated because you were lost in a group-mentality. Were you a fan at a sporting event? What was it?
|
|_____
|
|

Philip Zimbardo

Compliance

Consumer psychology

Obedience

Foot-in-the-door

Door-in-the face

Lowball technique

Cult

Pic 434: *Why* do you think the people "drank the kool-aid" (yes that is where that term came from)?

Pg. 435: Answer the questions on cults:

1

2

3

4

Stanley Milgram

People get fooled and manipulated all the time by salesmen, whether they be on TV or in real life. Or online. Or on the radio. Or on a billboard. All the time we are being sold goods and services that we may not need or even want. There is indeed a joy to sales-resistance, however, and if you know the tricks, you may be less apt to fall for one. Give 3 examples of the following:

Foot-in-the-Door trick   *Door in the face trick*   *Lowball trick*

1

2

3

Pic 436: In Milgram's experiment, the teacher who was giving the shocks was faced with this view:

15 volts	*75 volts*	*135 volts*	*195 volts*	*255 volts*	*315 volts*	*375 volts*	*450 volts*
Slight	Moderate	Strong	Very Strong	Intense	Extreme Intensty	Danger! Severe	XXX
O	O	O	O	O	O	O	O

Evaluate and be truthful: How far do you think you would have gone in the experiment? Circle the last button you would have pushed to shock the learner who got the multiple choice memory question wrong.

Pg. 438 M/C: write the answer in the form of a statement. Underline the letter answer.

1.

2.

3.

4.

5.

"Why did you punch that guy in the face?" "Central Route-Persuasion. It's basic psychology!"

Social cognition

Attitude

In the ABC Model of Attitudes, note the relevance of each of the ABC components:

Affective   *Behavior*   *Cognitive*

Chart 440: Relate the example used in the chart as an illustration of the ABC components (you can do it horizontal or vertical, whichever you wish):

Pic 440: What is the lesson here about the persuasiveness of the "be good to the environment- buy organic foods" ad campaign?

_____

What 'convinces' you to eat the foods you eat when you have a choice in the matter? How do you pick?

_____

Attitude formation

Summarize the importance of the various influences on attitude:

Direct contact   *Direct instruction*   *Interaction with others*   *Vicarious conditioning*

Persuasion

Note the four factors important in predicting how successful a persuasive effort at attitude adjustment might be:

Item   Reason

1)

2)

3)

4)

Elaboration likelihood model

Central route persuasion

Peripheral route persuasion

Pic 442: These jurors seen here may be persuaded via the peripheral-route by the lawyers trying to convince them they should vote a certain way. What kind of peripheral things may distract them?

Cognitive dissonance

Which of the following is an example of cognitive dissonance that has affected you in school?

a. I learned in school that there is no right or wrong, only conditioned responses, yet I think some things are just plain wrong no matter what.

b. School teaches me group interaction is more important that self-reliance, and tells me consensus is more important than principle, but I don't agree and think I'm right and able on my own- and the group is wrong.

c. All ethics are situational, they say, and there are no moral absolutes, but I think there are.

d. "There are no guilty people, only victims," my counselor says. But I would be mad if someone stole my wallet.

Self-perception theory

Pg. 444 M/C: write the answer in the form of a statement. Underline the letter answer.

1.

2.

3.

4.

5.

"I'm about to make the Fundamental Attribution Error, and you ain't gonna like it."

Impression formation

Pic 445: How are these Chinese jobseekers advertising their worthiness for an interview using knowledge of impression formation?

It is, as a general rule, better to dress for the job

a. you have   b. you used to have   c. you want

_____

Primacy effect

Social categorization

Labeling

Stereotyping

Which do you subscribe to more: *a. stereotypes may exist for a reason*   *b. stereotyping is never okay*

Implicit personality theory

IAT

Attribution theory

Situational cause

Dispositional cause

Fundamental attribution error

Give three examples of the F.A.E., noting if it is one in which you participated or were affected by:

1   2   3

Actor-observer bias

Pg. 446 M/C: write the answer in the form of a statement. Underline the letter answer.

1.

2.

3.

4.

5.

"Wait- are you discriminating against me because I am prejudiced, or are you prejudiced against me because I discriminate?"

Prejudice
_____

Discrimination
_____

Pic 450: Which was the integration of this Arkansas high school- by force- in 1957 trying to end?

     a. prejudice   b. discrimination

If you lived in Mexico, and many people in a town were against having Americans in their local school, what would you do?

     a. try to integrate   b. stay at my own school

Ethnocentrism
_____

In-groups
_____

Out-groups
_____

How many 'in-groups' (which are defined against other out-groups) can you think of regarding your own social identity? Make a quick list (yes, gamer counts if you define yourself as one):

Scapegoating
_____

Comic 451: What is this cartoon a metaphor for?

Pic 451: Can you think of any groups that are *not* ethnocentric?

Social cognitive theory
_____

Realistic conflict theory
_____

Jane Elliot
_____

Pg. 452: *Brown Eyes, Blue Eyes* began as an experiment that began 40 years ago on elementary school kids in Iowa, and is still being revised and applied to new populations today (*Youtube: Jane Elliot* to see how she is still doing it). Read and answer the questions below:

1

2

3

4

Social identity theory

Give an example to illustrate each of the following:

Social cognitive theory:

Realistic conflict theory:

Social identity theory:

Social identity

Describe and give examples of the three aspects of social definition in social identity theory:

Social categorization *Identification* *Social Comparison*

Stereotype vulnerability

Pic 453: What do you think each of these girls are thinking?

Girl on far left *Girl center left* *Girl center right* *Girl on far right*

Self-fulfilling prophecy

Pic 454: Do you recall when you had intergroup contact with someone who changed your views about that group?

"Robber's Cave"

Jigsaw classroom

Pg. 449 M/C: write the answer in the form of a statement. Underline the letter answer.

1.

2.

3.

4.

5.

"Your lips are venomous poison"   *-Alice Cooper*

Interpersonal attraction

Note the issues surrounding each of the following factors of attraction:

Physical   *Proximity*   *Similarity*   *Reciprocity*

Mere exposure effect

Complementary qualities

Pg. 458: Facebook and social networking has changed the search for "love". Read and answer:

1

2

In Sternberg's theory of love, discuss the role of the following components:

Intimacy   *Passion*   *Commitment*

Love triangle

Romantic love

Companionate love

Pg. 460 M/C: write the answer in the form of a statement. Underline the letter answer.

1.

2.

3.

4.

5.

*"Let's get started on this section boys and girls." **I SAID LET'S GET STARTED NOW!!!!!!!!!!!!!!!!!!!!!!!***

Aggression

Frustration-Aggression hypothesis

What have the following had to say about aggression:

Sigmund Freud   *Konrad Lorenz*   *Modern approaches*

How do the following affect aggression?

Testosterone   *Alcohol*

Pic 463: What have the following taught us about aggression?

Zimbardo Prison Experiment   *Abu Gharib Prison*

Social role

Media violence

Altruism

Prosocial behavior

Bystander effect

Diffusion of responsibility

Social neuroscience

Pg. 468 M/C: write the answer in the form of a statement. Underline the letter answer.

1.

2.

3.

4.

5.

Multiple Choice: Write the answer in the form of a statement, underlining the letter.

1.

2.

3.

4.

5.

6.

7.

8.

9.

FRQ.

_____

_____

_____

_____

_____

_____

_____

_____

_____

_____

_____

Mom, can your superego please stop telling my id how to behave? My own superego is bad enough. Dang.

Personality _____

Temperament _____

Character _____

How did the ancient Greeks and Romans, such as Hippocrates (the first scientific doctor) and Galen (a Roman anatomist) think about the origins of a person's personality?

_____

Scanning pg. 476, can you see how each of the modern psychological approaches has countered with its own theory?

a. yes I can   b. yes, I'm starting to

Summarize the four major perspectives on personality developed over the past century:

Psychodynamic	*Behaviorist*	*Humanistic*	*Trait*

What factors do you think have shaped *your* personality?

_____

Pic 477: What did Freud try to ascertain from patients who reclined on his famous couch?

_____

Freud's book, in which the claimed that Victorian-era Europeans had neuroses because they were too sexually frustrated, was called:

_____

Do you agree with Freud's main theory, presented in *Civilization and its Discontents,* that "The repression of sex, so apparent as an aspect of Western culture [during Freud's life], is the source of art, love and even civilization itself. However, neurosis and unhappiness are the price to be paid for these traits because neurosis and unhappiness are the inevitable result of repressing sexual urges."

_____

Unconscious mind _____

Id _____

Pleasure principle _____

Ego _____

Reality principle

Superego

Conscience

Pic 478: Sketch the Iceberg model of Freud's personality theory and label the parts:

Defense mechanisms

Table 480: Note the defense mechanisms, defining them and providing an example:

1

2

3

4

5

6

7

8

9

10

Psychosexual stages

Fixation

Oral stage   (age):

Anal stage   (age):

Anal expulsive personality _____

Anal retentive personality _____

Phallic stage _____ **(age):**

Penis envy _____

Castration anxiety _____

Oedipus complex _____

Electra complex _____

Latency stage _____ **(age):**

Puberty _____

Genital stage _____ **(age):**

On a 1-10 scale, how much of what you have just read about Freud's stages do you find disturbing?

You're not alone. Because his Austrian colleagues argued he was trying to subvert European culture with psychoanalysis, some called Freud's work "Jewish science" (Freud and most of his clients were Jewish). They used this as a term of derision. Others were angered he was labeling everything a psychosexual pathology, as in the case of Dora:

_____

"Freud used psychoanalysis to pathologize female resistance to male sexual advances. This is apparent in the famous analysis of the teenage Dora, who rejected the advances of an older married man. Dora's father sent her to Freud because he wanted her to accede to the man's advances as an appeasement gesture because the father was having an affair with the man's wife. Freud obligingly attributed Dora's rejection to 'repression of amorous desires' toward the man. The message is that 14-year-old girls who reject the sexual advances of older married men are behaving hysterically" (MacDonald 2003, 130).

Do you agree with psychologists who question the entire scientific basis of psychoanalysis?

| What evidence from the reading might someone questioning the scientific basis of Freud's theory use to demonstrate their position?

Psychoanalysis _____

Neo-Freudians _____

Carl Jung _____

Note the differences between the personal and collective unconscious in Jung's theory:

_____

Jung was a creative early psychoanalyst who broke away from Freud and went on his own. He looked at human societies and notice people follow archetypical patterns. Jungian psychologist Carl Golden on the website *Soulcraft* defines it like this: "The term 'archeype' has its origins in ancient Greek. The root words are 'archein' which means 'original' or 'old'; and 'typos' which means 'pattern, model or type'. The combined meaning is an 'original pattern of which all other similar persons, objects or concepts are derived, copied, modeled or emulated.'" Do archetypes, such as "the innocent, the regular guy/gal, the hero, the caregiver, the explorer, the rebel, the lover, the creator, the jester, the sage, the magician and the ruler" make sense to you from the long-term perspective of human development? What functions might they have?

Alfred Adler

Inferiority complex

Karen Horney

Basic anxiety

Neurotic personality

Pic 483: Which way might this boy be using to deal with anxiety? _____

Looking around at society today, and contrasting the norms and values of today with those of a century ago, evaluate the extent to which Freud's project to pathologize Victorian society was successful:

    a. very successful   *b. somewhat successful*   *c. unsuccessful*

Pg. 485 M/C: write the answer in the form of a statement. Underline the letter answer.

1.

2.

3.

4.

5.

6.

7.

8.

9.

10.

After all, everyone had got one of them, or so we was meant to believe

Habits

Question 486: How do you think a pattern of rewarding certain behaviors might end up becoming part of someone's personality pattern? What is that person perhaps seeking, from a behaviorist standpoint?

Social cognitive learning theorists

Social cognitive view

Albert Bandura

Reciprocal determinism

Self-efficacy

Chart 487: Sketch out the chart, being sure to include arrows pointing both ways to emphasize the reciprocal nature of the influences:

Locus of control

Pic 488: What is happening to this happy young lady's perception of locus of control?

Comic 488: What is it about behaviorism in general that these dogs are grumbling about?

Video Ad 479: In which approach to psychology does free will exist?   *a. behaviorism   b. humanistic*

Expectancy

Humanistic perspective

Carl Rogers

Self-actualizing tendency

Self-concept

Real self

Ideal self

Chart 489: Draw the venn diagram below, in which each area is about equal in size. Then, actually answer the basic humanistic questions in the following way: (Left area) – who you *want* to be, ideally, but have not yet achieved. (Center area) – aspects of you, your personality, your status in life, that have already achieved which match your loftiest, ideal self. (Right area) – aspects of you today that 'need improvement' because they do not match your ideal self:

Positive regard

Unconditional positive regard

Pic 490: What are the parents doing to "give unconditional positive regard"?

If she would have failed at what she was trying to do, say by wiping out while ice skating around the pond, would her parents have criticized her if using UPR?

Conditional positive regard

Fully functioning person

Positive psychology

Pg. 491 M/C: write the answer in the form of a statement. Underline the letter answer.

1.

2.

3.

4.

5.

TRAIT THEORIES NAME_____

What traits do you look for in a personality?

Trait theories _____

Trait _____

Gordon Allport _____

Surface traits _____

Source traits _____

Video ad 492: Copy the traits as you see them and then mark where you, in a self-evaluative way, say you are on the continuum:

==============================

==============================

==============================

==============================

==============================

==============================

==============================

==============================

==============================

==============================

==============================

==============================

==============================

==============================

==============================

Pic 493: Use the caption here and the text to summarize the strengths correlated with various traits:

Factor analysis

Graph 493: Sketch out the five-factor model and note the characteristics associated with them

High scorer characteristics	*Factor*	*Lower scorer characteristics*
	O	
	C	
	E	
	A	
	N	

Define each of the OCEAN terms to round out our study of trait theories today:

O

C

E

A

N

Trait-situation interaction

Pg. 495 M/C: write the answer in the form of a statement. Underline the letter answer.

1.

2.

3.

4.

5.

Do good and bad personalities really come from what kind of jeans you have?

Twin studies

Adoption studies

Current findings

Pic 496: What can we conclude about nature and nurture from the story of Jim Lewis and Jim Springer, who were wombmates but not roommates?

_____

_____

Graph 497: Generalize about the findings shown on the graph:

_____

_____

_____

Heritability

James Springer/James Lewis

Cultural personality

Operationally define the traits used in the four dimensions by Hofstede in his survey of personalities:

Individualism-Collectivism   *Power Distance*

Masculenity-Femininity   *Uncertainty Avoidance*

Questions 499:

    1)

    2)

Table 499: Which types of assessment are likely to be used by the following kinds of therapist:

Psychoanalyst   *Behaviorist*   *Humanist*   *Social-Cognitive*   *Trait*

Interview _____

Halo effect _____

Projective test _____

Rorschach inkblot test _____

Pic 501: As the psychologist asks the patient what he sees, what else is the psychologist looking for?

_____

_____

Sketch out the inkblot you see in mini-me form:

What do _you_ see?

_____

_____

TAT _____

Pic 501 (bot.): What does this story suggest to you? _____

Who is the person? _____ Why is he climbing? _____

Subjectivity _____

Direct observation _____

Rating scale _____

Frequency count _____

Personality inventory _____

Validity scales _____

MBTI _____

MMPI _____

Pg. 505 M/C: write the answer in the form of a statement. Underline the letter answer.

1.

2.

3.

4.

5.

Multiple Choice: Write the answer in the form of a statement, underlining the letter.

1.

2.

3.

4.

5.

6.

7.

8.

9.

FRQ.

_____

_____

_____

_____

_____

_____

_____

_____

_____

_____

_____

_____

ABNORMAL PSYCHOLOGY NAME_____

Is this assignment, for example, abnormal?

Abnormal behavior _____

Psychopathology _____

Trephining _____

Humors _____

Maladaptive behavior _____

Exorcism _____

Medical model _____

Prognosis _____

Etiology _____

Situational context _____

Subjective discomfort _____

Maladaptive _____

Pic 514: Why would most people in America consider this person 'abnormal' in a park or in the grocery store but not in front of a tax office or on the 4th of July?

_____

_____

What, in your view, is 'normal?' Can it be defined?   Are you 'normal' by your own standards?

_____   _____

Luckily, psychologists have developed five criteria to use when determining abnormality. Note them:

1

2

3

4

5

_____

Psychological disorder

Abnormality

Insanity

Insanity defense

Summarize how the biological model puts forth medical causes for psychological disorders:

Summarize what the following psychological models attribute psychological disorders to:

Psychodynamic   *Behaviorism*   *Cognitive*

Hiding problems

Learning problems

Thinking problems

Summarize what the sociocultural perspective attributes psychological disorders to:

Cultural relativity

Cultural syndromes

Biopsychosocial model

Summarize how the biopsychosocial perspective
Is a synthesis (or, 'all-of-the-above):

| Pic 516: How does this finding point to a
| cultural syndrome?
|
|
|
|

Taijin-kyofu-sho

Susto

Amok

Anorexia

Questions 517:

1

2

Pg. 518: About how many disorders are listed in the DSM-5?   What does DSM stand for again?

_____   _____

Summarize the types of disorders found in the following:

Axis I	*Axis II*	*Axis III*

Note the pros and cons of labeling:	*Pros*	*Cons*

Table 520: Note the major divisions of disorders, the specific disorders, and the known percentages:

Category	*Specific disorder*	*Percentage of population*

Pg. 521 M/C: write the answer in the form of a statement. Underline the letter answer.

1.

2.

3.

4.

Getting nervous? Just think what the morning of the AP test will be like! (Youtube: Skeletor laugh)

Pic 522: Answer the question on if you ever felt like this and when:

Teachers must be amazing! They give presentations like this every day and are never nervous! What's going on?

_____/_____

a. they are amazing
(you might want to put this just because)

*b. people get nervous in front of **peers***
(would you be nervous in front of elementary kids?)

Anxiety disorders

Free floating anxiety

Phobia

Note the meaning of the following phobias and the legitimate *reason* people fear these things in a usual way- which sometimes are exaggerated to an irrational degree and are labeled a maladaptive phobia:

Agoraphobia   *Claustrophobia*

Meaning

Reason

Acrophobia   *Odontophobia*

Meaning

Reason

Hemaphobia   *Arachnophobia*

Meaning

Reason

Ophidiophobia   *Xenophobia*

Meaning

Reason

Pic 523: Recalling that phobias are regular fears taken to an irrational degree, can you say for certain whether this lady is afraid of heights to the point of being acrophobic? Why or why not?

Social anxiety disorder

Panic attack

Panic disorder

GAD

Provide an example of real circumstances that might trigger:

      Social anxiety   *Panic attack*   *Generalized anxiety*

OCD

Define and provide an example of the kinds of things the 'obsessive' aspect of OCD entails versus the 'compulsive' aspect:

                Obsessions   *Compulsions*

Pic 524: What is this person doing that can be considered compulsive?

Does that say Hoville 6 mi. away? Hopefully they mean the place the Grinch visits at Christmastime.

Pic 525: What % of people claimed stress? _____

ASD

PTSD

Is PDSD limited to veterans of the military who, while on active duty, experienced trying times or singular shocks while in combat?

Have you known anyone who has PTSD? _____

What was the reason? (If not, put N/A):

Magnification

All-or-nothing thinking

Overgeneralization

Minimization

Spectrum 527: Delineate and label (and color?) the range of emotions of the following continuum:

===

Affect

Mood disorders

Major depressive disorder

Bi-polar disorder

Seasonal affective disorder

Manic

Draw a Venn diagram and label the left bubble 'major depressive disorder,' the central bubble 'both' and the right bubble 'bi-polar disorder'. Fill it in:

ADHD

Pic 529: There is a huge controversy about how far to medicate kids identified as ADHD. What do you think ADHD kids should receive:

 a. nothing   *b. extra time on school work*   *c. medicine to keep them quiet and relaxed*

Pg. 531 M/C: write the answer in the form of a statement. Underline the letter answer.

1.

2.

3.

4.

5.

6.

7.

8.

9.

10.

Now don't get no dissociative disorder just 'cause were talkin' 'bout all this bad mood stuff

Dissociative disorders
_____

Dissociative amnesia
_____

Fugue state
_____

Blackout
_____

DID
_____

Multiple personalities
_____

Depersonalization disorder
_____

Pic 533: Oh wait there is no pic. Or comic. Or chart. Or graph. Or table. Or anything. Do you think the publishers just got lazy?

_____

Have you seen a TV show, movie, or read a comic or book in which a character had more than one personality?

_____

_____

Psychology in the News 534: Read Sybil's story and answer the questions:

1

2

Pg. 535 M/C: write the answer in the form of a statement. Underline the letter answer.

1.

2.

3.

4.

5.

*If the book people can be lazy, can we be lazy too? _____

"Well I've got antisocial personality disorder, but most of the time it stays quiet." -Worst job interview answer... ever

Schizophrenia _____

Psychotic _____

Delusions _____

Note the manifestations and symptoms of the following dilusions:

      Delusions of persecution   *Delusions of reference*

      Delusions of influence   *Delusions of grandeur*

_____

Clanging _____

Word salad _____

Hallucinations _____

What are some common hallucinations that people afflicted with schizophrenia have reported?

_____

Flat affect _____

Catatonia _____

Pic 536: Who is John Nash and what was his contribution to the psychology and economics?

Positive symptoms _____

Negative symptoms _____

Pic 538: What happened to Nathaniel Ayers?

_____

Stress-vulnerability model

Chart 538: Based on this data, summarize some conclusions on the relationship of genetics to schizophrenia. Pretend you are explaining it to the spouse of a person just diagnosed:

| Pic 539: Note the specific finding neuroscientists have managed to make using this technology:

| _____

| In people with schizophrenia:

| _____

Personality disorders

ASPD

Some symptoms of ASPD include:

| Name some movie villains who you would diagnose as afflicted with ASPD:

Sociopath

Psychopath

Borderline personality disorder

Pg. 541 M/C: write the answer in the form of a statement. Underline the letter answer.

1.

2.

3.

4.

5.

Multiple Choice: Write the answer in the form of a statement, underlining the letter.

1.

2.

3.

4.

5.

6.

7.

8.

9.

FRQ.

_____

_____

_____

_____

_____

_____

_____

_____

_____

_____

"You're about to be treated. And you might not like it. And it might not help." Ow.

Where was Bedlam and why is it (in)famous?

_____

Pic 548: Would Dr. Philippe Pinel have approved of Bedlam? How do you know?

_____

What were Dorothea Dix' contributions to to how patients are treated nowadays?

_____

What kinds of nasty things went away with these reforms?

_____

Therapy _____

Eclectic _____

Psychotherapy _____

Action therapy _____

Insight therapy _____

Biomedical therapy _____

Psychoanalysis _____

Dream interpretation _____

Review the differences between manifest content and latent content:

   Manifest   *Latent*

_____   _____

Free association _____

Resistance _____

Transference _____

Pic 551: Note the differences in how psychodynamic therapy is done today from the psychoanalysis of yesteryear. What changed?

Why is the term 'client' now preferred to 'patient'?

Directive vs. nondirective _____

Person-centered therapy _____

Authenticity _____

UPR _____

Empathy _____

Reflection _____

Pic 552: If this therapist were using UPR, would his expression change if this client told him the following: "Doc I'll tell you, is the importance of a comma. At a meeting of psychologists, people were introducing themselves to each other and saying what fields they worked in. Two people near me smiled and shook hands. One said, 'I'm Étienne, a clinical psychologist from Paris,' in a funny accent. The other person answered, 'Glad to meet you, I am Rhonda, a psychotherapist from Cleveland.' Then they turned to me, who wasn't invited, who was just there with my nun-chucks looking like I like didn't fit in. I guess they didn't want to be unprofessional, so they disregarded these concerns. Étienne introduced himself and asked me about my field, and I said, 'French? You sound more Italian saying all, 'Hey, I'm-a-tan,' and pretty darn arrogant. Heck, I got a tan too. What's my field? I'm a psycho, therapist.' That's when I started flailing my nun-chucks and everyone screamed."

a. yes   _b. no_

Motivational interviewing _____

Gestalt psychology _____

Hidden vs. denied past _____

Owning up _____

Pg. 555 M/C: write the answer in the form of a statement. Underline the letter answer.

1.

2.

3.

4.

5.

6.

7.

8.

9.

10.

"Aversion therapy? Oh yeah... this is the good stuff."

Behavior therapy
_____

Behavior modification
_____

Applied behavior analysis
_____

Systematic desensitization
_____

Table 557: One might think a fear of rabbits- cute little bunnies that is- is irrational. But recall the terrible tortures sometimes used by locking people in with starving rats and imagine it with starving rabbits- not pretty. If you still can't imagine it just imagine it is big nasty sewer rats not bunnies. Copy the systematic desensitization chart tracing the steps:

10-   60-

20-   70-

30-   80-

40-   90-

50-   100-

Aversion therapy
_____

Rapid-smoking technique
_____

Question 558: Think of four aversion therapies you would prescribe for four different phobias:

1)   2)

3)   4)

Exposure therapy
_____

VR therapy
_____

Flooding
_____

EMDR
_____

Modeling
_____

Participant modeling
_____

Reinforcement
_____

Token economy

Contingency contract

Extinction

Time-out

Pic 559: What in this time-out area makes it less of a punishment chamber of doleful rumination and more of a place where the young mind may wander upon flights-a-fancy?

_____

Cognitive therapy

Aaron Beck

Summarize the contents of the following distortions of thought as outlined by Beck's Cognitive Therapy:

	Meaning	*Example*
Arbitrary inference		
Selective thinking		
Overgeneralization		
Magnification vs. minimization		
Personalization		

CBT

Note the three basic goals of CBT:

1

2

3

Note the two irrational belief examples and then think of a third that would fit:

1

2

3

Table 562: Note the characteristics of psychotherapies:

Type/people	Goal	Methods

Group therapy

Family counseling

Pic 562: Would you like to go to one of these family counseling sessions? _____

Self-help group

Support group

Pic 563: Why do people attend self-help meetings?   Name three self-help groups:

_____   _____

Pg. 565 M/C: write the answer in the form of a statement. Underline the letter answer.

1.

2.

3.

4.

5.

"Even if you evaluate our sessions poorly, you still have to pay. That's the good part."

Hans Eysenck

What did Eysenck's buzz-kill findings reveal in the 1950s?

Pic 566: This comic warns us that 'curing' all manner of psychological diversity may result in:

    a. total normalcy   *b. regression to the mean*   *c. a degree of boredom*   *d. all of these*

Note some of the shortfalls in studying the effectiveness of psychotherapies:

| Answer Question 566: How does one with
| a problem know what kind of therapist to go to?
|
|
|
|
|

Common factors approach

Note the relevance of the following items to studying psychotherapies' effectiveness:

    Protected setting   *Opportunity for catharsis*

    Learning new behaviors   *Practicing new behaviors*

Evidence-based practice

Evidence-based treatment

Comic 567: What is the meaning of the paradisiacal scenery in the background in this cartoon?

Questions 568: Read and answer the questions about mental health on campus:

1

2

Barriers to psychotherapy

Cybertherapy

Shh... no questions this time. Don't tell the teacher.

When all else fails, use drugs*

Biomedical therapy _____

Psychopharmacology _____

Antipsychotic drugs _____

Table 571: Ah tables. You will miss them when this year is done, you know that. This is the last one! Savor it:

Classification	Treatment areas	Side effects	Examples
1)			
2)			
3)			
4)			
5)			
6)			
7)			

Tardive dyskinesia _____

Antianxiety drug _____

Benzodiazepines _____

Mood-stabilizer _____

Antidepressant drug _____

Note some common examples of the following:

Antianxiety drugs	*Mood-stabilizing drugs*	*Antidepressant drugs*

Electroconvulsive therapy

Pic 575: How does ECT work?

_____

_____

Would you volunteer to be administered ECT if asked to?

_____

When is ECT actually used on people?

_____

_____

Psychosurgery

Lobotomy

Pic 576: What happened to poor Rosemary Kennedy?

_____

_____

Pic 576 (bot.): What kinds of symptoms would rTMS be employed to treat?

_____

Bilateral anterior cingulotomy

Lesioning

Pic 578: What is a virtual reality environment, like the one shown here, actually like?

_____

Virtual reality

"The more I hear about e-school the more I like the idea. You know, maybe it's time we bought virtual reality headsets. That way students could come to school, get some food, then have teachers pipe lessons into their helmets with less distraction than exists in a regular classroom setting, what with other students around. Now it will be a totally isolated, personal environment. They could have those special gloves that air-type, and turn in skills-based items via email. They could be enhanced with Wii-type accessories, and could participate in the Model-UN kind of fishbowl without any social anxiety issues, via avatar. They could play jeaopardy-type games like Kahoot, all right there in their VR mask. They could get instant feedback on objective knowledge tests. Punishment or reward would be immediate. As time went on and the school aged, we could take it down and put up a large Wal-Mart-style box, so everyone would be able to walk around an aisle-path, thus exercising while learning. Kinesthetics achieved. Eventually, it could all be run automatically."

Do you think this is a good idea for the future of schooling? _____

Pg. 574 M/C: write the answer in the form of a statement. Underline the letter answer.

1.

2.

3.

4.

5.

*prescribed by a certified psychiatrist for a legitimate reason

Multiple Choice: Write the answer in the form of a statement, underlining the letter.

1.

2.

3.

4.

5.

6.

7.

8.

9.

FRQ.

_____

_____

_____

_____

_____

_____

_____

_____

_____

_____

_____

Applied psychology _____

Psychiatric social worker _____

Psychiatrist _____

Psychologist _____

Ph.D _____

Psy.D _____

Clinical psychology _____

Counseling psychology _____

Developmental psychology _____

Experimental psychology _____

Social psychology _____

Personality psychology _____

Physiological psychology _____

Neuropsychology _____

Comparative psychology _____

Health psychology _____

Educational psychology _____

School psychology _____

Sports psychology _____

I/O psychology _____

Forensic psychology _____

Community psychology _____

Environmental psychology _____

Multiple Choice: Write the answer in the form of a statement, underlining the letter.

1.

2.

3.

4.

5.

6.

7.

8.

9.

10.

You have hereby completed the curriculum.

Part II

Extra Resources

Crash Course Guide

Reviewer _____

It's Review Time!

Topic of today's episode _____

Preview: From my memory logs about what we have been talking about this week, I predict Hank Green will be talking about topics like:

_____

Some things he covered that were not in the book or talked about in class were:

_____

What silly (or not so silly) gimmicks did Mr. Green have this time?

_____

How did those items or gimmicks tie-in to the material in the chapter?

_____

_____

After Watching:

a) Was there a 'deep' lesson at the very end? What was it?

b) To me, the most interesting part of this chapter (the thing most relevant to my life), is _____ because:

Test Correction Guide

Time to get it right!

Corrector_____

Test Name_____

Directions: Identify the numbers of the answers you got wrong on the test and write them:

Number   **Page in Book**   **Correct answer (written in the form of a statement using stem of question)**

_____

_____

_____

_____

_____

_____

_____

_____

_____

_____

_____

_____

_____

_____

_____

_____

_____

_____

_____

_____

I got most of these wrong because…

Psych Movie Review

Reviewer _____

What chapter in the book is this movie most appropriate for? _____

The topic(s) it cover(s): _____

Identify some of the key characters in the movie that embody psych concepts in the chapter. Describe how their psychological issue(s) affect the storyline in the early part of the film.

_____

_____

_____

_____

What was the "low point" for the main character(s) in the movie? Did the psych issue cause that low point / crisis to occur?

_____

_____

By the end of the movie, it is probable that whatever crises or effects the psychological issue was causing was resolved in some way. Explain how this turn of events came about:

_____

_____

_____

Rate this movie from 0-3: _____
3: it was intellectually stimulating and entertaining
2: it had good points but was rather dull
1: it seemed misleading or irrelevant
0: it was not worth seeing- waste of time

One image or scene that stuck out was:

_____

_____

Why did you rate it the way you did?

_____

_____

Would you recommend this movie to
Friends or relatives outside of psych class?

_____

_____

_____

Psych Documentary Review   Reviewer _____

What chapter in the book is this documentary most appropriate for? _____

What topics does it cover? _____

According to the documentary, what are some old and new breakthroughs and discoveries in this particular field of psychological research? What implications does the new research hold?

OLD   **NEW**

How does the material presented in this documentary piece affect your life or the lives of people around you? Do you see yourself making any material changes to your life as a result of what this documentary has been discussing?

_____

_____

Rate this documentary from 0-3: _____
3: it was intellectually stimulating and informative
2: it had good points but was rather dull
1: it seemed misleading or irrelevant
0: it was not worth seeing- waste of time

Why did you rate it the way you did?

_____

_____

One image or scene that stuck out was:

_____

_____

_____

Why do you think this particular scene was more memorable than the rest?

_____

_____

_____

Any final thoughts on this documentary?

Yale Lecture Review

Reviewer _____

Verify the right lecture to see with this chapter.
Go to http://antarcticaedu.com/opencourses.htm, and click on Bio Science. Click on the first one under Psychology, the 'Yale' lectures, and make your selection.

Prof. Bloom is talking to college students who are somewhat familiar with the basic concepts in each chapter. His lectures are meant to illustrate the concepts. Review the vocab for the chapter you are working in first.

What topics does Prof. Bloom discuss in this lecture? Which concepts does he use to discuss those topics, and what examples does he use? You should note at least three topics, and at least ten concepts and examples for a full lecture. Use the vocabulary where appropriate.

TOPICS   CONCEPTS   EXAMPLES

How did Prof. Bloom's lecture change or influence the way you think about these topics?

Psychsim Tie-Ins to Ciccarelli & White

Week 1: chapter 1: history, approaches   Psychology's Timeline

Week 2: chapter 1: scientific attitude

Week 3: chapter 1: data collection   Descriptive Statistics

Week 4: chapter 1: correlation, experiments   Correlation, What's Wrong with this Study

Week 5: chapter 2: neurons   Neural Messages

Week 6: chapter 2: brain   Hemispheric Specialization, Dueling Brains

Week 7: chapter 2: brain, genes   Brain and Behavior

Week 8: chapter 3: sensation, eye   Colorful World

Week 9: chapter 3: other senses, perception   Visual Illusions, Auditory System

Week 10: chapter 4: consciousness, sleep, dreams   EEG and Sleep Stages

Week 11: chapter 4: hypnosis, drugs   Your Mind on Drugs

Week 12: chapter 5: classical conditioning   Classical Conditioning, Maze Learning

Week 13: chapter 5: operant conditioning   Operant Conditioning, Helplessly Hoping, Monkey See, Monkey Do

Week 14: chapter 6: memory   Iconic Memory, Short Term Memory, Forgetting, Trusting Your Memory, When Memory Fails

Week 15: chapter 7: cognition, language   My Head is Spinning

Week 16: chapter 7: intelligence   Get Smart

Week 17: chapter 8: childhood development   Conception to Birth, Cognitive Development

Week 18: chapter 8: adult development   Who Am I?, Signs of Ageing

Week 19: chapter 9: motivation   Hunger and the Fat Rat, Catching Liars

Week 20: chapter 9: emotion   Expressing Emotion

Week 21: chapter 10: stress   All Stressed Out

Week 22: chapter 10: social influence

Week 23: chapter 11: conformity, obedience   Everybody's Doing It, Social Decision Making

Week 24: chapter 11: groups, discrimination

Week 25: chapter 11: attraction, aggression, altruism   Dating and Mating, Not My Type

Week 26: chapter 12: Freudian personality

Week 27: chapter 12: trait theories, other   Mind Reading Monkeys

Week 28: chapter 13: anxiety disorders   Mystery Client

Week 29: chapter 13: mood disorders, other   Losing Touch with Reality

Week 30: chapter 14: psychotherapies   Computer Therapist

Week 31: chapter 14: biomedical therapies   Mystery Therapist

*You can access these lab tutorials by Googling: MyersAP1e (or if you want the added ones for the second edition then MyersAP2e). You can also access more by Googling: Psychinquiry.

Direct URL for Psychsim is: http://bcs.worthpublishers.com/myersap2e/default.asp

Direct URL for Psychinquiry is: http://ebooks.bfwpub.com/psychinquiry

Extra Weekly Projects

WEEK 1: Have students break into groups and have each group make a poster looking at a psychological topic from a certain perspective (i.e.: psychoanalytical, behaviorist)... Locate and watch the first 45 min. of Charles Osgood's *In Search of Ourselves*. You might also do the Introspection activity, where a piece of candy is distributed and students write their sensory reactions to the candy in as much excruciating detail as possible. You also may do the 'Dinner with a Dead Psychologist' activity, in which students pair up and report what questions they determined to ask the psychologist, and how they think he or she would answer them. View Crash Course Psychology episode #1.

WEEK 2: Do the Outrageous Celebrity project, whereby students examine the behaviors/motivations of a notorious figure in the public spotlight, and try to explain their attitudes and actions from a specific psychological approach, or a combination of many. Examples abound, Lady Gaga is a popular one, Dennis Rodman (though a bit dated), etc. Have them collect images of their transformation to outrageousness. Ask them to rationalize the behavior/attitude as well. How might Freud explain it vs. Skinner, Rogers, Beck or Bandura? Have them construct a three-pronged biopsychosocial chart for it at the end. Do the Psychsim Lab: Psychology's Timeline (see addendum for website addresses). Psychsim goes with another textbook but anyone can access the labs (seach: MyersAP2e and hit worksheets, print out the worksheet and give to students, then have them log onto that site and hit the corresponding tutorial- tutorial means lab in this case).

WEEK 3: Have students brainstorm what research method (survey, case study, naturalistic observation, etc.) would be most appropriate for actual inquiries into some psychological or social phenomena. Examine pitfalls in survey questions, like bias, complex wording, etc. Students might also do naturalistic observation in the cafeteria at lunch. If you have Bolt's resource binder (or if you don't, have students make a list of all the presidents of the USA and their age at inauguration)- and then have them make a bar graph of all the presidents inaugurated in their 40's, 50's, 60's and 70's. Then have students calculate the mean age, median age and the mode. Get a clip of James Randi challenging Yri Geller on his spoon bending on the Tonight Show with Johnny Carson to illustrate the scientific attitude. Carl Sagan was a big proponent of this as well, and you can see it on Youtube's *The Sagan Series*. Do Psychsim Lab: Descriptive Statistics.

WEEK 4: If you have the Bolt binder (and if not your school should buy it for you- search: Bolt Psychology Resource Binder), do the Nuts and Bolts demonstration to illustrate data collection, the Yardstick experiment to demonstrate experimenter bias (when you cheat and let the boy win, then claim boys have better reflexes), and the correlation project with hair length in inches vs. number of shoes owned, to demonstrate how to place data on a scatterplot (and the concept of confounding variables due to the fact that the long hair did not *cause* the number of shoes to go up). Something else did. You could do hair loss vs. years of marriage too, 'find a correlation,' and use the data to bolster your false hypothesis that too much commitment makes a guy's hair fall out! Studies show... Finally, looking at ethics issues in experiments of the past is a good platform for debate on what should be allowed to happen for the good of psychological science. Search for notorious experiments in the history of psychology as a guide. If you want some entertainment you can look into serious ethics violations like stolen cadavers (Hare, Burke, Knox case), and have students identify why this experiment wouldn't pass committee peer review today. Crash Course Psychology episode #2. Psychsim Lab: Correlation and Psychsim Lab: What's Wrong with this Picture.

WEEK 5: Take time to diagram a neuron on the board, draw it out with the students and label each part, describe its function, and run a simulation from dendrite to the release of neurotransmitters into the next synaptic gap. You could do the 'Neuron Dance' where students line the back of the room holding one-another's forearms and cannot 'activate' until the previous neuron had 'fired.' One at a time, the students 'fire' and move their arms in a wave pattern. You may have them not touch each other to simulate the synaptic gap. The film *Awakenings* with Robin Williams and Robert de Niro goes with this section. You might also show the clip of Lou Gehrig giving his famous "Luckiest Man" speech after being diagnosed with the mysterious disease called MS. Search for articles on oxytocin by Nicholas Wade and Kevin MacDonald for the 'revenge of biology' perspective. Crash Course Psychology episode #3. Psychsim Lab: Neural Messages.

WEEK 6: Take time to diagram the whole brain on the board, starting with 'lower brain', then limbic system, then cerebellum, then the cerebral cortex. Emphasize the corpus callosum as an 'east-west' nerve highway from right to left hemispheres, and the thalamus as a 'north-south' nerve highway from lower to upper brain. Students may jigsaw a brain part, one for each or one per peer-group, and then discuss its function and significance in psychology. The Wagner Preference Inventory can be done to see which hemisphere, if any, the survey taker favors. Watch Yale lecture #2. Crash Course Psychology episode #4. Psychsim Lab: Brain and Behavior, Hemispheric Specialization and Dueling Brains.

WEEK 7: Talking about psychology from the evolutionary perspective can take many forms. If you are daring, you can mention E.O. Wilson's *Sociobiology* and how much controversy it caused in the 1970s and 80s at the apex of environmentalism. You can mention Charles Murray and Richard Herrnstein's *The Bell Curve* and the controversy it caused in the 1990s, the controversy surrounding psychologists Richard Lynn, J. Philippe Rushton and Kevin MacDonald in the 2000s, and Satoshi Kanazawa, Nicholas Wade, Frank Salter, and DNA discoverer James Watson in the 2010s. Have students pick a trait people have, from tendency to cooperate to aggression to care for young to various phobias, and determine likely reasons that particular trait exists as it does in people today. What was/is its survival value? Also, with Nature-Nurture, have students evaluate how much of height (90%), intelligence (75%) and personality/character (50%) is inherited vs. from environment. You may also discuss a recent article on selecting the traits of babies, increasingly offered by labs at home and abroad. Genetic modification is an underlying theme in the movie *Starship Troopers,* which portrays a society in which eugenic selection of human beings has been implemented. High school students run genetic scans on each other as if it were a game, and the results compare boys and girls, and give them a 'genetic compatibility score,' which students will find interesting. Watch Yale lecture 10. Psychsim Lab: Mind Reading Monkeys. No Crash Course for this week.

WEEK 8: Students can brainstorm times they did bottom-up vs. top-down processing. You can diagram the eye in detail on the board, imagining a light wave's journey to transduction and the journey of the impulse to the feature detectors and visual cortex- and students could copy it on a blank piece of paper, perhaps color-coding it. The book *Teaching Tips for General Psychology* has a few good ideas for sensation. Crash Course Psychology episodes #5 and 6. Psychsim Lab: Colorful World.

WEEK 9: Using brain teasers and visual illusions readily findable online, have students determine which parts of the sense and perception process the illusions are 'fooling', or it may be a concept they are illustrating. People will not all formulate the same perception, so you can talk about 'truth' as an absolute value vs. being relative to what someone perceives, i.e.: 'in the eye of the beholder.' Is there anything we know is true cognitively that we do not perceive as such? You could also find a magic trickster or card dealer who tricks perceptions, or use the video of the woman sauntering across a basketball game with an umbrella (or in another variation in a gorilla suit). If you like, have students sketch out the ear, and compare what happens to a sound wave with what happens to a light wave. When does transduction occur? Etc. Yale lecture 7, 11 and guest lecture 1 are appropriate this week. Crash Course Psychology episode #7. Psychsim Lab: Visual Illusions and Auditory System.

WEEK 10: Taking a graphic journey of a night's sleep on the board, hour by hour and cycle by cycle, is an informative way to teach the waves, states and circadian rhythm. Have students recall their dreams and write them, then look for common themes and things that happen in dreams, and discuss whether Freud was right about manifest and latent content. Give the Morningness-Eveningness Questionarire to see if the person is a night owl or a morning lark. Movies about sleep and dreams include *Inception* and *Total Recall.* Yale lecture 17 works here. Crash Course Psychology episodes #8 and 9. Psychsim Lab: EEG and Sleep Stages.

WEEK 11: With drugs you can assign groups to investigate different ones, and report to the class. The class can classify it, see the negative side yet also the motivation people have to abuse it. Be sure to make clear the different forms of addition, and connect it to all the biopsychosocial reasons people use, legally and illegally. 'Spiders on Drugs' is a humorous Youtube video if there are 5 extra minutes. If you can, get a cop to come in and give a presentation on what drugs do to the community you live in. If you want to make an even stronger point about this section, you could do the Icekube Addiction activity by Charles Blair-Broeker, whereby students have to keep ice in its solid form around them throughout the day, and you are their "dealer" with a large supply in your room. They fiend for it and have to get out of class or lunch or anything, just to get their fix from you- and hide their problem from others- an apt simulation of addiction. Movies? We should mention movies about alcohol and drug addiction. There are a lot of them but a few stand out. *The Lost Weekend* about alcohol addition (1945) is one. The movie won the Oscar for best director and best actor. Find it on Youtube or Amazon. In *28 Days*, Sandra Bullock plays an alcohol addict in rehab, demonstrating the therapy process. *Trainspotting, Blow, Easy Rider, The Doors* and *Requiem for a Dream* are movies about drug addiction. The Star Trek: The Next Generation episode *The Game* looks at addiction to a game, an 80s premonition of our own addictions to virtual realities, one of which being video games. Crash Course Psychology episode #10. Psychsim Lab: Your Mind on Drugs.

WEEK 12: Youtube videos of the Pavlov and Watson experiments are good follow-ups to the classical conditioning discussion. A clip from *The Office* TV show (search Jim conditions Dwight) is a humorous short. Have students think about other times they and people in general are classically conditioned. Take the Sensitivity to Punishment and Reward Questionnaire. Yale lecture 3 is appropriate this week. Crash Course Psychology episode #11. Psychsim Lab: Classical Conditioning and Maze Learning.

WEEK 13: Youtube videos of the Thorndike Puzzle Box and Skinner Pigeon experiments are helpful, along with a humorous clip from Big Bang Theory (Search: Big Bang Theory Conditioning) where the friend does operant conditioning on the girlfriend of his roommate. Have students figure out what reinforcement schedules are used in a variety of cases (i.e.: gambling is variable ratio, conditioning Penny with chocolate candies is fixed ratio). If it happens to be Thanksgiving or Christmas break, or if you are willing to spend two class periods on a full-length movie, *Bedtime for Bonzo* (1951) examines the Nature-nurture issue at the height of behaviorism. Ronald Reagan stars as Professor Boyd, who wants to marry the daughter of the dean, and the dean finds out Boyd's dad was in jail- an indication Boyd had criminal genes he doesn't want in his family. The bad old nature guy finally comes around to the power of environment at the end, but with a few twists that students love. This movie is cheap on *Amazon*. An article on observational learning and the latest on how TV/movie/video game violence affects kids would work here. Find Amy Sutherland's NY Times article *What Shamu Taught me about a Happy Marriage* and have students marvel at a lady who did operant condition on her husband as if he were a circus animal… and it worked. Yale lecture 4 is appropriate this week. Crash Course Psychology episode #12. Psychsim Lab: Operant Conditioning, Monkey See, Monkey Do, and Helplessly Hoping.

WEEK 14: Have students graph 1-6 on the x-axis and 0-18 on the y-axis. Do the demo where they pair up and one has six trials of 10 seconds each to memorize a random 18-digit number you put on the board in big font. Cover it with the screen or something else after each 10-second viewing. The learners then speak the number back to the recorder, and the recorder marks how many were spoken back correctly, between 0 and 18. This well-used demo is very good because it can illustrate many of the concepts in 7a, like serial position effect, etc. Also, do the Seven Dwarves recall game.

Give them 30 seconds to write all the names they remember, and in round two speak out the names of 20, including 13 false names you make up like 'Slappy' or 'Tired.' Then have them get the concepts of recall vs. recognition, and why fill in the blank tests are harder than multiple choice. You can also do the demo on words related to sleeping and nighttime, available in Bolt's binder. For flashbulb memories, try having them think of their own, and also things for different generations in history, i.e.: Pearl Harbor, JFK blown away, Apollo Moon landing, 9/11, etc. If you'd like to see a movie for this section, try *Memento, Fifty First Dates, Limitless, Finding Nemo, Robocop, the Bourne Identity, The Butterfly Effect,* or *The Notebook* (Alzheimer's disease). Yale lecture 8 is appropriate this week. Crash Course Psychology episodes #13 and 14. Psychsim Lab: Iconic Memory, Short Term Memory, Forgetting, Trusting Your Memory and When Memory Fails.

WEEK 15: Bolt's binder has a good one on problem solving that is also online if you don't have the binder. Students like the Buddhist Monk Problem, the Truthtellers and Liars Problem, and the Hobbits and Orcs problem. For language, there is an opportunity to read a review of Pinker's *The Language Instinct* and then Theodore Dalrymple's *The Gift of Language,* which argues against some of Pinker's claims about facility for language being mostly inborn. Star Trek: The Next Generation tackled miscommunication in *Darmok,* an episode when the crew meets an alien race that speaks in metaphors, not in semantic structures familiar to humans. An assignment to this episode is included in the addendum. You can find clips on Youtube or watch the whole thing. The movie *Good Will Hunting* involves a gifted person being discovered by psychology professionals and channeled into realizing his potential. Yale lecture 6 is appropriate this week. Crash Course Psychology episodes #15 and 16. Psychsim Lab: My Head is Spinning.

WEEK 16: If doing an actual IQ test, the Wechsler is a good choice because it is for adults. Debating the effectiveness of standardized testing as an indicator of future success in college, or for comparison with others or for a job is a good idea. Testing the Sternberg creative and practical intelligences is effective too, as is testing the Gardner multiple intelligences and taking emotional intelligence surveys. The WWI Intelligence Test is humorous, and the Culture-Fair Intelligence test is eye-opening. *Forrest Gump* shows us that high I.Q. doesn't necessarily mean happy, in its portrayal of an intellectually disabled man whose innocence and naivety in a tough world is heartwarming. Crash Course Psychology episode #23. Psychsim Lab: Get Smart. Do the Griggs "One-Minute Intelligence Test." Telling students about MENSA and giving them a MENSA admissions test is possible this week. They are usually intrigued by a society for 'the highly intelligent,' and like seeing videos of MENSA gatherings across the world. This is also a good counterbalance to the thorny issue of group differences in intelligence that appears at this point, highlighted in many politically incorrect but difficult to dismiss articles on the Internet, notably by La Griffe du Lion, an anonymous statistician, at http://lagriffedulion.f2s.com/. If you want to cause controversy, you could present stats from Charles Murray's *Human Accomplishment,* a book that found that over 90-percent of the significant figures in all the arts and sciences of the world for the last 2,500 years, were both white and male. As you might imagine, this caused a backlash and could trigger debate in your class as well as to if, how and why. Yale 13 works here. Crash Course episode #24.

WEEK 17: Discuss the stages of prenatal development- there are plenty of clips for this- and the Piaget stages. If your school can afford it, obtain *Inside Out Psychology,* a video series featuring David Myers and a whole host of top psychologists. Warning: it is expensive. Have students note the key changes and abilities in each Piaget stage, and debate whether stage theories are valid models of human development on the escalator vs. stairs comparison. You can have students recall scenes and events that made impressions on them in each year of their childhood, from 3 on. Have them reflect on what they thought about, their moral standing if they had one, and what they were interested in (motivation) in each grade. Call it "The Years of Life" or something like that. Give them the Parental Authority Questionnaire Pertaining to Mothers to see if they can identify their mom's parenting style. *Breakfast Club* is a movie showing the teenage identity crisis. Yale lecture 5 is good here. Crash Course Psychology episodes #18 and 19. Psychsim Lab: Conception to Birth and Cognitive Development.

WEEK 18: *The Real Roots of the Midlife Crisis* by Rouch in *The Atlantic* examines that secular malady in which people wake up one day and ask "is this all there is?" If you are brave, you can show clips from *American Beauty* when Kevin Spacey manifests symptoms of a midlife crisis. Have students ponder what might give them a midlife crisis if they do not accomplish it. Have them fill out the Life/Values/Goals survey, imagining they are on the verge of finishing their time as fellow travelers on the Spaceship Earth, which gets them thinking. *What Dreams May Come* is about coming to terms with death, while Yale does a class on dying, findable online at: http://antarcticaedu.com/opencourseengineering.htm. Yale lecture 12, 15 fits here. On Youtube, search *Coronet "Self-Conscious Guy"* and see the identity issue, followed by *"Psychological Maturity: Act Your Age,"* and *"How Friendly are You?"* for a 1950s perspective. Older adulthood is portrayed in the film *Grumpy Old Men.* Crash Course Psychology episode #20. Psychsim Lab: Who am I? and Signs of Ageing.

WEEK 19: If you or your class is shy, this is not your chapter. It has Freud's psychosexual stages, discussions of the incidence of homosexuality, the sex motivation of males for spreading their DNA around to as many different nubile females as possible, and the motivation for females to secure comfort and prosperity by ensnaring an alpha male. How to approach it? Focus on hunger and the hypothalamus messing with the body's equilibrium! You can also look at how advertising motivates us to buy stuff we probably don't need. There is a good sheet on this in the *Teaching Tips for General Psychology* book. Give students the Exploration Inventory, and have them assess where they are on Maslow's hierarchy, relating it to motivations in their present day. If you are interested in gender, sexual orientation and identity, *The Birdcage* takes a humorous look at how heterosexual and homosexual people see each other, while *What Women Want* looks at how men and women see each other differently. A movie for eating disorders is *Girl, Interrupted.* Yale lecture 14 and guest lecture 2 are appropriate this week. Another movie worth seeing for the post-Freud Psychodynamic school is *Finding Joe,* about heroism and overcoming personal troubles through tapping into the Jungian archetype present but partially hidden within oneself. This is presented through an analysis of the teachings of Joseph Campbell, the foremost mythologist of the 20th century. You can also Youtube his videos series called *The Power of Myth,* which covers many topics. Crash Course Psychology episodes #17, 27 and 33. Psychsim Lab: Hunger and the Fat Rat, and Catching Liars.

WEEK 20: Debating the three theories is a good start, but find online the reasons each group of theorists obtained their opinion on the matter. Ekman's universal expressions data is watchable on Youtube, and a good talk can be based on what each emotion conveys worldwide, and which ones differ by culture or country. Happiness and how to obtain it can be found in documentaries on Youtube and Netflix. The *Star Trek* episode *The Enemy Within* can be found to show the captain becoming two people, one full of raw emotion and the other without enough of it, a yin-yang situation. Consequences ensue and the moral is that a healthy balance is best. A clip about Phineas Gage is appropriate here. Give the Need for Affect Scale to check their level of proneness to emotionality. On Youtube, get a 1950s perspective on emotions by searching: *Psychology Coronet.* This company made school documentaries that are informative for us today because they give a window into how things were different. Students like the one called "Controlling Your Emotions," as well as "Understanding Emotions" and "Overcoming Fear." Crash Course Psychology episode 25. Psychsim Lab: All Stressed Out.

WEEK 21: Finally, National Geographic's *Portrait of a Killer,* is a good look at Robert Sapolsky's work fin iguring out how stress hurts us over time. Do the *Psychinquiry* lesson on Stress Level at: http://ebooks.bfwpub.com/psychinquiry. Yale lecture 9 and 10 are appropriate this week. Crash Course Psychology episodes #25. Psychsim Lab: Expressing Emotion.

WEEK 22: Social Psych material abounds. You'll want to show clips of Asch's conformity experiment and Milgram's Obedience experiment on Youtube. The British recreation of Milgram is good. Yale episode 16 works here. Crash Course Psychology episode #37. Psychsim Lab: Social Decision Making.

WEEK 23: Show documentaries on Zimbardo's prison experiment and possibly The Wave, which wraps together all three: conformity, obedience and deindividuation. Yale episode 16 works here. Crash Course Psychology episode #38. Psychsim Lab: Everybody's Doing It.

WEEK 24: If you want to extend the conformity, obedience, role adoption theme, you can hit Jane Elliott's *Brown Eyes, Blue Eyes* experiment from the 1960s, and then watch the Youtube clip *How Racist are You* (search with Elliott as a keyword) to see the modern application of the technique in Britain. You can also watch the German version of *The Wave,* called *Die Welle,* but you may have to buy it on Amazon. Students can compare it to both the American version and the actual case.

WEEK 25: You might look at cooperation and altruism through the lens of Game Theory, as well as present the Prisoner's Dilemma. For love, one can take the Love Styles Quiz online. One may also take any number of Social Attitudes quizzes or prejudice or tolerance inventories. If you want to watch another movie for this material, *Lord of the Flies* fits the bill, covering role assumption, aggression and prejudice, while finding the meaning in life and happiness is the theme in *Dead Poets' Society.* Crash Course Psychology episodes #39 and 40. Psychsim Lab: Dating and Mating, and Not My Type.

WEEK 26: Students can analyze examples of all the Freudian defense mechanisms and explain what is going on and why. Teacher Kelly Cavanaugh had a good activity for defense mechanisms, in *Teaching Tips for General Psychology.* She has her students watch an episode of *Frasier* called *Frasier's Edge,* season 8, episode 12. If you find it on Netflix or Youtube, you can play it and students can identify when the main character, Frasier, a psychiatrist who has a midlife crisis, invokes the defense mechanisms. This takes 20 min, and students like seeing the last moment in human history before cell phones became ubiquitous and instant communication the norm. Crash Course Psychology episode #21.

WEEK 27: This is the chapter of surveys and personality inventories. Students can take any you choose, and then examine and compare results, and hopefully plot them somehow on a continuum or chart. Bolt's binder has at least 20. Others are online, like the Social Styles inventory, featuring driver, expressive, amiable and social, used by businesses for the last couple decades. You might also have them do the Gregorc Mind Styles inventory. OCEAN spectrum inventories like the BFI are effective and engaging this week, as are clips of stereotypical personalities and type A, type B behavior. View the Ted Talks on introverts by Susan Cain. Crash Course Psychology episode #22.

WEEK 28: Bolt's binder has surveys for nearly all of the maladies in this section, including various anxiety disorders. Students can take them and see how they fit among the groups that have taken them. Warn them they are not to self-diagnose with the surveys, so they don't all leave thinking they have an acute case of OCD or PTSD. Discuss a self-made list of various phobias, and be sure to include *nomophobia,* the phobia of being disconnected from one's social network. OCD themes run through *As Good as it Gets, Matchstick Men* and *The Aviator.* PTSD is a theme in *Rambo: First Blood* and *Apocalypse Now.* Crash Course Psychology episodes #28 and 29. Psychsim Lab: Mystery Client.

WEEK 29: Psychopathy and sociopathic behavior is no happy topic, but looking at actual psychopathic cases might be a good idea, to see how far the range of human mental maladies can stretch. There are enough cases, sadly, that each student may be able to produce a different case study. If you want to watch a movie, then *Rain Man* is appropriate for this chapter as it deals with

Savant Syndrome. *Fight Club* deals with Dissociative Identity Disorder and insomnia. In *Miracle on 34th Street,* a man who believes he is Santa Claus brings Christmas cheer to some New Yorkers in the 1940s. He is promptly sent to a psychologist who says he is delusional. In *Zoolander* and *Mean Girls,* people suffer from narcissistic personality disorder. Many of the villains from the 25+ James Bond movies are good examples of antisocial personality disorder, as is Hannibal Lecter in *Silence of the Lambs. Hamlet,* in any of its incarnations, is a good example of Major Depressive Disorder. Beethoven's story in *Immortal Beloved* may count for bi-polar disorder, its up to you. The *Star Trek* episode *The Conscience of the King* brings up issues of antisocial personality disorder. Yale 18 fits here. Crash Course Psychology episodes #30, 31, 32, and 34. Psychsim: Losing Touch with Reality.

WEEK 30: Psychotherapy. Get a Ted Talks with Philip Zimbardo called "The Demise of Guys." This wonders how to use therapy to treat video game / dirty movies addiction in males that may be interfering with their social lives and making them depressed (not to mention girls unhappy). You might follow it with an Internet or social network addiction survey. A humorous movie called *Anger Management* looks at group therapy, and *One Flew Over the Cuckoo's Nest* shows institutionalization. Yale episode 19 fits here. Crash Course Psychology episode #35. Psychsim Lab: Computer Therapist (tell students it's a real person on the other end and see how long it takes them to figure out they are not instant messaging).

WEEK 31: Biomedical therapy is controversial in some cases. Watch the Frontline episode *The Medicated Child,* read Theodore Dalrymple's articles *An Ill for Every Pill* and *Forced Smiles* about Prozac. On the other hand, watch the movie *A Beautiful Mind* to see the wonders and pitfalls of biomedical therapies like Thorazine for schizophrenia, a malady that can hardly be treated without a biomedical intervention. Review the plot of the book *Brave New World,* where a drug called Soma, something like Xanax mixed with Prozac, is used to keep everyone docile, content and… obedient. *Breaking Bad* is a TV series about a high school chemistry teacher whose environment and circumstances change, helping turn him into a producer of crystal meth as he struggles with reconciling his humanity with an emerging antisocial personality disorder, while *Dexter* is a TV series about a sympathetic serial killer. Yale episode 20 works here. Crash Course episode #36. Psychsim Lab: Mystery Therapist.

Summer Assignment

AP PSYCHOLOGY SUMMER ASSIGNMENT

*** You'll need your own lined paper to do this assignment ***

GO TO ANTARCTICAEDU.COM/PSY.HTM AND CLICK ON THE GROOVIEST MOST FAR OUT WEBSITE (2ND ONE DOWN). Click "Want to Score a 5" and then on "Trippy Text"

This site was put together by AP Psych teachers and is a good source that will remain with us all year as we study our 14 chapters (one every two weeks).

1-7. Click Introduction and read through it. On a separate sheet of paper, discuss in complete short answer sentences the seven schools of psychology and how they would explain aggression in people (like Stewie from Family Guy). How would they diagnose or figure out what is wrong with him? What would be their object of investigation?

When done with 1-7, go back and click on Psychoanalytic School. This is Freud's way of doing psychology from the 1920s.

8-10. On your paper, discuss (8) the id, ego and superego, (9) what free association is, and (10) how Freud has been criticized. Click back and go to Behavioral School.

11-13. On your paper, discuss (11) what classical conditioning is, (12) what operant conditioning is, and (13) what observational learning is. Go back and hit Cognitive School.

14-16. On your paper, discuss (14) the perspective of the cognitive school, (15) Ellis' contributions (theories/discoveries) and (16) Beck's contributions. To back to Humanistic.

17-20. On your paper, discuss (17) what determinism is, (18) what freewill is, and (19) which one you agree with more: the Behaviorists that say our behaviors are determined by the environment around us, or the Humanists who say we have the freewill to dominate the environmental forces acting on us. Please give an example from your own life of how you or someone you know either was 'controlled' by their environment, or 'controlled' it. (20) Draw Maslow's Hierarchy of Needs and label it. Go back and hit Biological School.

20-22. From the perspective of Neuroscience: (20) what are three places our emotions/feelings come from? (21) Draw a neuron and label it. (22) Describe what each part you labeled does in one sentence. Go back and go to Cognition.

23-27. What (23) are the 4 kinds of cognition (mental activity) we will study? (24-27) Introduce (summarize) each of them- what are they? Go back and hit Abnormal.

28-34. Make a list (28) of anxiety disorders and look it up online (ex. Wikipedia page). Describe each disorder and name a famous person who have been diagnosed with that disorder. Do the same with (29) somatoform disorders, (30) dissociative disorders, (31) mood disorders, (32) personality disorders, (33) schizophrenia, and (34) the 'others'.

35. Go to psychmovies.com and look through the list of movies about psychology. Make a list of up to 5 that you have seen OR would like to see.

You're done! Have a great rest of the summer, and if you have any questions, send me an email at:

Best Bets Online

<u>All of the following are indexed for convenience at Antarcticaedu.com/psy.htm</u>

Kahoot.it can be a fun review game. Make a free account and the students can compete using their smartphones. Search for AP Psych jeopardy-style quizzes.

Appsychology.com is a very good site with an informal, accessible style. Students can use it as a summary of the chapters in the text and for review.

Psychologytoday.com magazine has a whole lot of articles on most subjects, and a database of local psychologists for most metropolitan areas. Students can search for them by zip code, and see what fields they specialize in. Have students find things to read by hovering over 'topics' or using the search box.

On CharlieRose.com, a famed interviewer talks to people working in psychology (as well as most other fields) and you can search by topic.

Ted.com/talks has psych related speakers.

Look for prison psychologist Theodore Dalrymple's articles on City Journal, New English Review and The Spectator magazine. Everything he writes is worth reading.

The Ciccarelli and White's *Psychology* AP edition book site has content that can be accessed if you have the right passwords and login name.

For more labs, try PsychInquiry as a search term, and a whole index will come up that you can select from. http://ebooks.bfwpub.com/psychinquiry/

On Youtube, search for Crash Course Psychology for reviews, as well as the many clips suggested above and others. You can download the video if your school blocks Youtube, and bring the clips in on an external hard drive.

As Myers and Ciccarelli & White are the most widely used textbooks now, and have been for a generation, which textbooks were most popular two and three generations back? In the 1950s when behaviorism was at its height, it was Engle's *Psychology* (1957), and later, at the cusp of the neuroscience revolution, it was Ragland and Saxon's *Invitation to Psychology* (1985). Both of these books cost about 5 bucks on Amazon, and for perspective's sake are probably worth obtaining.

===

Thank You!

If this resource book has no use for you, it has no value. We strive to make materials you can actually *use*. <u>No waste</u>, no filler, only usable resources with minimal marginalia aligned with the course for convenience. This is how the *Tamm's Textbook Tools* system works:

Coursepak A, the one you already have, has daily assignments for Monday and Tuesday (or two other days of the week, however you work it). It has the vocab, people and chapter work covered.

Coursepak B, also available on *Amazon* and elsewhere, has material that can be used other days during the week. This time the focus is reading comprehension, online activities, short answers and free response questions (FRQs). Sometimes these take the form of document analysis (DBQs) and other AP* and AP* Psych specific formats.

Coursepak C, *The Grand Tour* series, is the part of the *Tamm's Textbook Tools* line that stretches across the disciplines. If you were interested in psychology, you would look for *The Grand Tour of Psychology*. If you were doing a world history class, you'd look for *The Grand Tour of World History*. All *Grand Tours* weave in material from a variety of subjects in the way your subject relates to them. By presenting the big moments in the history and development of the subject, math and science are discussed in social studies courses, pleasing the cross-curricular team-teaching types. Each big moment is presented and students are asked to respond objectively at times, subjectively at other times. Additionally, care has been taken to ensure the *Grand Tour* series are done in a way that makes students feel like they are part of the great conversation, with the overall aim of kindling (or rekindling) excitement for the topic in a way that is aligned with the curriculum. 'Fun' isn't the right word- meaningful is. Bringing down-to-earth meaning back to the social sciences is the highest aim of this series.

Made in the USA
Columbia, SC
04 June 2019